The Westminster Shorter Catechism

Copyright © 2020 Berenice Aguilera
All rights reserved.
ISBN: 9798375271439
All verses taken from the King James Bible

The Westminster Shorter Catechism

The original text of 1647, with the Assembly's proof texts.

AGREED UPON BY THE ASSEMBLY OF DIVINES AT WESTMINSTER, WITH THE ASSISTANCE OF COMMISSIONERS FROM THE CHURCH OF SCOTLAND, AS A PART OF THE COVENANTED UNIFORMITY IN RELIGION BETWIXT THE CHURCHES OF CHRIST IN THE KINGDOMS OF SCOTLAND, ENGLAND, AND IRELAND. AND APPROVED ANNO 1648, BY THE GENERAL ASSEMBLY OF THE CHURCH OF SCOTLAND, TO BE A DIRECTORY FOR CATECHISING SUCH AS ARE OF WEAKER CAPACITY,

WITH THE PROOFS FROM THE SCRIPTURE .

Assembly at EDINBURGH, July 28, 1648. Sess. 19.

Act approving the SHORTER CATECHISM

The General Assembly having seriously considered the SHORTER CATECHISM agreed upon by the Assembly of Divines sitting at Westminster, with assistance of Commissioners from this Kirk; do find, upon due examination thereof, that the said Catechism is agreeable to the word of God, and in nothing contrary to the received doctrine, worship, discipline, and government of this Kirk: And therefore approve the said Shorter Catechism, as a part of the intended uniformity, to be a Directory for catechising such as are of weaker capacity.

A. KER.

(ALL IMAGES & IMAGE TEXT IS COURTESY OF WIKIPEDIA)

*Study to shew thyself approved unto God,
a workman that needeth not to be ashamed, rightly
dividing the word of truth.*

2 Timothy 2:15

CONTENTS

Introduction..1
   Q. 1. What is the chief end of man?..3
   Q. 2. What rule hath God given to direct us how we may glorify and enjoy him?..3
   Q. 3. What do the Scriptures principally teach?............................3
   Q. 4. What is God?..3
   Q. 5. Are there more Gods than one?..4
   Q. 6. How many persons are there in the Godhead?....................4
   Q. 7. What are the decrees of God?...4
   Q. 8. How doth God execute his decrees?...................................4
   Q. 9. What is the work of creation?...4
   Q. 10. How did God create man?...4
   Q. 11. What are God's works of providence?...............................6
   Q. 12. What special act of providence did God exercise towards man in the estate wherein he was created?....................................7
   Q. 13. Did our first parents continue in the estate wherein they were created?..7
   Q. 14. What is sin?..7
   Q. 15. What was the sin whereby our first parents fell from the estate wherein they were created?..8
   Q. 16. Did all mankind fall in Adam's first transgression?............8
   Q. 17. Into what estate did the fall bring mankind?......................8
   Q. 18. Wherein consists the sinfulness of that estate whereinto man fell?...8
   Q. 19. What is the misery of that estate whereinto man fell?.........9
   Q. 20. Did God leave all mankind to perish in the estate of sin and misery?..9
   Q. 21. Who is the Redeemer of God's elect?................................9
   Q. 22. How did Christ, being the Son of God, become man?......10
   Q. 23. What offices doth Christ execute as our Redeemer?.........11
   Q. 24. How doth Christ execute the office of a prophet?............11
   Q. 25. How doth Christ execute the office of a priest?...............11

Q. 26. How doth Christ execute the office of a king?................12
Q. 27. Wherein did Christ's humiliation consist?.......................12
Q. 28. Wherein consisteth Christ's exaltation?...........................12
Q. 29. How are we made partakers of the redemption purchased by Christ?...12
Q. 30. How doth the Spirit apply to us the redemption purchased by Christ?...13
Q. 31. What is effectual calling?..13
Q. 32. What benefits do they that are effectually called partake of in this life?..13
Q. 33. What is justification?..13
Q. 34. What is adoption?..15
Q. 35. What is sanctification?...15
Q. 36. What are the benefits which in this life do accompany or flow from justification, adoption, and sanctification?..................15
Q. 37. What benefits do believers receive from Christ at death?. 15
Q. 38. What benefits do believers receive from Christ at the resurrection?..17
Q. 39. What is the duty which God requireth of man?................17
Q. 40. What did God at first reveal to man for the rule of his obedience?...17
Q. 41. Wherein is the moral law summarily comprehended?......17
Q. 42. What is the sum of the ten commandments?....................18
Q. 43. What is the preface to the ten commandments?...............19
Q. 44. What doth the preface to the ten commandments teach us? 19
Q. 45. Which is the first commandment?...................................19
Q. 46. What is required in the first commandment?...................19
Q. 47. What is forbidden in the first commandment?.................19
Q. 48. What are we specially taught by these words before me in the first commandment?..20
Q. 49. Which is the second commandment?..............................20
Q. 50. What is required in the second commandment?...............20
Q. 51. What is forbidden in the second commandment?.............20

Q. 52. What are the reasons annexed to the second commandment?...23
Q. 53. Which is the third commandment?...................................23
Q. 54. What is required in the third commandment?....................23
Q. 55. What is forbidden in the third commandment?.................23
Q. 56. What is the reason annexed to the third commandment?. .23
Q. 57. Which is the fourth commandment?.................................24
Q. 58. What is required in the fourth commandment?.................24
Q. 59. Which day of the seven hath God appointed to be the weekly sabbath?...24
Q. 60. How is the sabbath to be sanctified?................................24
Q. 61. What is forbidden in the fourth commandment?...............25
Q. 62. What are the reasons annexed to the fourth commandment?
....25
Q. 63. Which is the fifth commandment?....................................25
Q. 64. What is required in the fifth commandment?....................27
Q. 65. What is forbidden in the fifth commandment?..................27
Q. 66. What is the reason annexed to the fifth commandment?...27
Q. 67. Which is the sixth commandment?...................................27
Q. 68. What is required in the sixth commandment?...................27
Q. 69. What is forbidden in the sixth commandment?.................27
Q. 70. Which is the seventh commandment?...............................28
Q. 71. What is required in the seventh commandment?...............28
Q. 72. What is forbidden in the seventh commandment?.............28
Q. 73. Which is the eighth commandment?.................................28
Q. 74. What is required in the eighth commandment?.................28
Q. 75. What is forbidden in the eighth commandment?...............28
Q. 76. Which is the ninth commandment?...................................29
Q. 77. What is required in the ninth commandment?...................29
Q. 78. What is forbidden in the ninth commandment?.................29
Q. 79. Which is the tenth commandment?...................................29
Q. 80. What is required in the tenth commandment?...................29
Q. 81. What is forbidden in the tenth commandment?.................31
Q. 82. Is any man able perfectly to keep the commandments of

God?..31
Q. 83. Are all transgressions of the law equally heinous?............31
Q. 84. What doth every sin deserve?...31
Q. 85. What doth God require of us, that we may escape his wrath and curse, due to us for sin?..31
Q. 86. What is faith in Jesus Christ?..32
Q. 87. What is repentance unto life?..32
Q. 88. What are the outward and ordinary means whereby Christ communicateth to us the benefits of redemption?........................32
Q. 89. How is the Word made effectual to salvation?..................32
Q. 90. How is the Word to be read and heard, that it may become effectual to salvation?...33
Q. 91. How do the sacraments become effectual means of salvation?..33
Q. 92. What is a sacrament?...33
Q. 93. Which are the sacraments of the New Testament?............33
Q. 94. What is baptism?...36
Q. 95. To whom is Baptism to be administered?..........................37
Q. 96. What is the Lord's Supper?..37
Q. 97. What is required for the worthy receiving of the Lord's Supper?..37
Q. 98. What is prayer?..38
Q. 99. What rule hath God given for our direction in prayer?.....38
Q. 100. What doth the preface of the Lord's Prayer teach us?.....38
Q. 101. What do we pray for in the first petition?........................38
Q. 102. What do we pray for in the second petition?...................39
Q. 103. What do we pray for in the third petition?......................39
Q. 104. What do we pray for in the fourth petition?....................39
Q. 105. What do we pray for in the fifth petition?.......................39
Q. 106. What do we pray for in the sixth petition?......................40
Q. 107. What doth the conclusion of the Lord's Prayer teach us? 40
Footnotes...43

Introduction

The Westminster Shorter Catechism is a summary of the principles and beliefs of the Christian faith, in the form of questions and answers.

It was originally put together by an assembly of English and Scottish theologians and laymen in 1646.

In this version the questions and answers are presented with relevant verses below. At the back of the book the verses are written out in full for your convenience.

May this book bless you and give you greater knowledge and insight into the Christian faith.

Ralph Brownrigg (1592–1659) was bishop of Exeter from 1642 to 1659. He spent that time largely in exile from his see, which he perhaps never visited. He was both a Royalist in politics, and a Calvinist in religion, an unusual combination of the period. Brownrigg opposed Laudianism in Cambridge during the 1630s and at the Short Parliament Convocation of 1640. Nominated to the Westminster Assembly, he apparently took no part in it.

Q. 1. What is the chief end of man?

A. Man's chief end is to glorify God,[1] and to enjoy him forever.[2]
[1]. Ps. 86:9; Isa. 60:21; Rom. 11:36; I Cor. 6:20; 10:31; Rev. 4:11
[2]. Ps. 16:5-11; 144:15; Isa. 12:2; Luke 2:10; Phil. 4:4; Rev. 21:3-4

Q. 2. What rule hath God given to direct us how we may glorify and enjoy him?

A. The Word of God, which is contained in the Scriptures of the Old and New Testaments,[3] is the only rule to direct us how we may glorify and enjoy him.[4]
[3]. Matt. 19:4-5 with Gen. 2:24; Luke 24:27, 44; I Cor. 2:13; 14:37; II Pet.1:20-21; 3:2, 15-16
[4]. Deut. 4:2; Ps. 19:7-11; Isa. 8:20; John 15:11; 20:30-31; Acts 17:11; II Tim. 3:15-17; I John 1:4

Q. 3. What do the Scriptures principally teach?

A. The Scriptures principally teach, what man is to believe concerning God,[5] and what duty God requires of man.[6]
[5]. Gen. 1:1; John 5:39; 20:31; Rom. 10:17; II Tim. 3:15
[6]. Deut. 10:12-13; Josh. 1:8; Ps. 119:105; Mic. 6:8; II Tim. 3:16-17

Q. 4. What is God?

A. God is a Spirit,[7] infinite,[8] eternal,[9] and unchangeable,[10] in his being,[11] wisdom,[12] power,[13] holiness,[14] justice,[15] goodness,[16] and truth.[17]
[7]. Deut. 4:15-19; Luke 24:39; John 1:18; 4:24; Acts 17:29
[8]. IKings 8:27; Ps. 139:7-10; 145:3; 147:5; Jer. 23:24; Rom. 11:33-36
[9]. Deut. 33:27; Ps. 90:2; 102:12, 24-27; Rev. 1:4,8
[10]. Ps. 33:11; Mal. 3:6; Heb. 1:12; 6:17-18; 13:8; Jas. 1:17
[11]. Ex. 3:14; Ps. 115:2-3; I Tim. 1:17; 6:15-16
[12]. Ps. 104:24; Rom. 11:33-34; Heb. 4:13; I John 3:20
[13]. Gen. 17:1; Ps. 62:11; Jer. 32:17; Mat. 19:26; Rev. 1:8
[14]. Heb. 1:13; I Pet. 1:15-16; I John 3:3, 5; Rev. 15:4, 3:5, 26
[15] Gen. 18:25; Ex. 34:6-7: Deut. 32:4; Ps. 96:13; Rom 3:5,26
[16]. Ps. 103:5; 107:8; Matt. 19:17; Rom. 2:4
[17]. Ex. 34:6; Deut. 32:4; Ps. 86:15; 117:2; Heb. 6:18

Q. 5. Are there more Gods than one?

A. There is but one only,[18] the living and true God.[19]
[18]. Deut. 6:4; Isa. 44:6; 45:21-22; I Cor. 8:4-6
[19]. Jer. 10:10; John 17:3; I Thess. 1:9; I John 5:20

Q. 6. How many persons are there in the Godhead?

A. There are three persons in the Godhead: the Father, the Son, and the Holy Ghost;[20] and these three are one God, the same in substance, equal in power and glory.[21]
[20]. Matt. 3:16-17; 28:19; II Cor. 13:14; I Pet. 1:2
[21]. Ps. 45:6; John 1:1; 17:5; Acts 5:3-4; Rom. 9:5; Col. 2:9; Jude 24-25

Q. 7. What are the decrees of God?

A. The decrees of God are, his eternal purpose, according to the counsel of his will, whereby, for his own glory, he hath foreordained whatsoever comes to pass.[22]
[22]. Ps. 33:11; Isa. 14:24; Acts 2:23; Eph. 1:11-12

Q. 8. How doth God execute his decrees?

A. God executeth his decrees in the works of creation and providence.[23]
[23]. Ps. 148:8; Isa. 40:26; Dan. 4:35; Acts 4:24-28; Rev. 4:11

Q. 9. What is the work of creation?

A. The work of creation is, God's making all things of nothing, by the word of his power,[24] in the space of six days, and all very good.[25]
[24]. Gen. 1:1; Ps. 33:6, 9; Heb. 11:3
[25]. Gen. 1:31

Q. 10. How did God create man?

A. God created man male and female, after his own image,[26] in knowledge,[27] righteousness, and holiness,[28] with dominion over the creatures.[29]

[26] Genesis 1:27
[27] Colossians 3:10
[28] Ephesians 4:24
[29] Genesis 1:28;Psalm 8

Q. 11. What are God's works of providence?

A. God's works of providence are, his most holy,[30] wise,[31] and powerful[32] preserving[33] and governing[34] all his creatures, and all their actions.[35]

[30]. Ps. 145:17
[31]. Ps. 104:24
[32]. Heb. 1:3
[33]. Neh. 9:6
[34]. Eph. 1:19-22
[35]. Ps. 36:6; Prov. 16:33; Matt. 10:30

Q. 12. What special act of providence did God exercise towards man in the estate wherein he was created?

A. When God had created man, he entered into a covenant of life with him, upon condition of perfect obedience; forbidding him to eat of the tree of the knowledge of good and evil, upon the pain of death.[36]

[36]. Gen. 2:16-17; Jas. 2:10

Q. 13. Did our first parents continue in the estate wherein they were created?

A. Our first parents, being left to the freedom of their own will, fell from the estate wherein they were created, by sinning against God.[37]

[37]. Gen. 3:6-8, 13; II Cor. 11:3

Q. 14. What is sin?

A. Sin is any want of conformity unto, or transgression of, the law of God.[38]

[38]. Lev. 5:17; Jas. 4:17; I John 3:4

Jeremiah Burroughs (c. 1600 – 1646) was an English Congregationalist and a well-known Puritan preacher. He was a member of the Westminster Assembly and one of the few who opposed the Presbyterian majority. While one of the most distinguished of the English Independents, he was one of the most moderate, acting consistently in accordance with the motto on his study door (in Latin and Greek): "Opinionum varietas et opinantium unitas non sunt ασυστατα" ("Difference of belief and unity of believers are not inconsistent").

Q. 15. What was the sin whereby our first parents fell from the estate wherein they were created?

A. The sin whereby our first parents fell from the estate wherein they were created, was their eating the forbidden fruit.[39]

[39]. Gen. 3:6

Q. 16. Did all mankind fall in Adam's first transgression?

A. The covenant being made with Adam,[40] not only for himself, but for his posterity; all mankind, descending from him by ordinary generation, sinned in him, and fell with him, in his first transgression.[41]

[40]. Gen. 2:16-17; Jas. 2:10
[41]. Rom. 5:12-21; ICor. 15:22

Q. 17. Into what estate did the fall bring mankind?

A. The fall brought mankind into an estate of sin and misery.[42]

[42]. Gen. 3:16-19, 23; Rom. 3:16; 5:12; Eph. 2:1

Q. 18. Wherein consists the sinfulness of that estate whereinto man fell?

A. The sinfulness of that estate whereinto man fell, consists in the guilt of Adam's first sin,[43] the want of original righteousness,[44] and the corruption of his whole nature,[45] which is commonly called original sin; together with all actual transgressions which proceed from it.[46]

[43]. Rom. 5:12, 19
[44]. Rom. 3:10; Col. 3:10; Eph. 4:24
[45]. Ps. 51:5; John 3:6; Rom. 3:18; 8:7-8; Eph. 2:3
[46]. Gen. 6:5; Ps. 53:1-3; Matt. 15:19; Rom. 3:10-18, 23; Gal. 5:19-21; Jas. 1:14-15

Q. 19. What is the misery of that estate whereinto man fell?

A. All mankind by their fall lost communion with God,[47] are under his wrath[48] and curse,[49] and so made liable to all the miseries of this life,[50] to death[51] itself, and to the pains of hell forever.[52]

[47]. Gen. 3:8, 24; John 8:34, 42, 44; Eph. 2:12; 4:18
[48]. John 3:36; Rom. 1:18; Eph. 2:3; 5:6
[49]. Gal. 3:10; Rev. 22:3
[50]. Gen. 3:16-19; Job 5:7; Ecc. 2:22-23; Rom. 8:18-23
[51]. Ezek. 18:4; Rom. 5:12; 6:23
[52]. Matt. 25:41, 46; II Thess. 1:9; Rev. 14:9-11

Q. 20. Did God leave all mankind to perish in the estate of sin and misery?

A. God, having out of his mere good pleasure, from all eternity, elected some to everlasting life,[53] did enter into a covenant of grace to deliver them out of the estate of sin and misery, and to bring them into an estate of salvation by a Redeemer.[54]

[53]. Acts 13:48; Eph. 1:4-5; II Thess. 2:13-14
[54]. Gen. 3:15; 17:7; Ex. 19:5-6; Jer. 31:31-34; Matt. 20:28; I Cor. 11:25; Heb. 9:15

Q. 21. Who is the Redeemer of God's elect?

A. The only Redeemer of God's elect is the Lord Jesus Christ,[55] who, being the eternal Son of God,[56] became man,[57] and so was, and continueth to be, God and man in two distinct natures, and one person, forever.[58]

[55]. John 14:6; Acts 4:12; I Tim. 2:5-6
[56]. Ps. 2:7; Matt. 3:17; 17:5; John 1:18
[57]. Isa. 9:6; Matt. 1:23; John 1:14; Gal. 4:4
[58]. Acts 1:11; Heb. 7:24-25

Q. 22. How did Christ, being the Son of God, become man?

A. Christ, the Son of God, became man, by taking to himself a true body, and a reasonable soul,[59] being conceived by the power of the Holy Ghost, in the womb of the virgin Mary, and born of her,[60] yet without sin.[61]

[59]. Phil. 2:7; Heb. 2:14, 17
[60]. Luke 1:27, 31, 35
[61]. II Cor. 5:21; Heb. 4:15; 7:26; I John 3:5

Q. 23. What offices doth Christ execute as our Redeemer?

A. Christ, as our Redeemer, executeth the offices of a prophet,[62] of a priest,[63] and of a king,[64] both in his estate of humiliation and exaltation.

[62]. Deut. 18:18; Acts 2:33; 3:22-23; Heb. 1:1-2
[63]. Heb. 4:14-15; 5:5-6
[64]. Isa. 9:6-7; Luke 1:32-33; John 18:37; I Cor. 15:25

Q. 24. How doth Christ execute the office of a prophet?

A. Christ executeth the office of a prophet, in revealing to us, by his Word[65] and Spirit,[66] the will of God for our salvation.[67]

[65]. Luke 4:18-19, 21; Acts 1:1-2; Heb. 2:3
[66]. John 15:26-27; Acts 1:8; IPet. 1:11
[67]. John 4:41-42; 20:30-31

Q. 25. How doth Christ execute the office of a priest?

A. Christ executeth the office of a priest, in his once offering up of himself a sacrifice to satisfy divine justice,[68] and reconcile us to God,[69] and in making continual intercession for us.[70]

[68]. Isa. 53; Acts 8:32-35; Heb. 9:26-28; 10:12
[69]. Rom. 5:10-11; II Cor. 5:18; Col. 1:21-22
[70]. Rom. 8:34; Heb. 7:25; 9:24

William Bridge (c. 1600 – 1670) was a leading English Independent minister, preacher, religious and political writer and a member of the Westminster Assembly. There he was one of the Five Dissenting Brethren, the small group of leading churchmen who emerged at the head of the Independent faction, opposing the Presbyterian majority.

Q. 26. How doth Christ execute the office of a king?

A. Christ executeth the office of a king, in subduing us to himself, in ruling and defending us,[71] and in restraining and conquering all his and our enemies.[72]

[71]. *Ps. 110:3; Matt. 28:18-20; John 17:2; Col. 1:13*
[72]. *Ps. 2:6-9; 110:1-2; Matt. 12:28; I Cor. 15:24-26; Col. 2:15*

Q. 27. Wherein did Christ's humiliation consist?

A. Christ's humiliation consisted in his being born, and that in a low condition,[73] made under the law,[74] undergoing the miseries of this life,[75] the wrath of God,[76] and the cursed death of the cross;[77] in being buried, and continuing under the power of death for a time.[78]

[73]. *Luke 2:7; II Cor. 8:9; Gal. 4:4*
[74]. *Gal. 4:4*
[75]. *Isa. 53:3; Luke 9:58; John 4:6; 11:35; Heb. 2:18*
[76]. *Ps. 22:1 (Matt. 27:46); Isa. 53:10; I John 2:2*
[77]. *Gal. 3:13; Phil. 2:8*
[78]. *Matt. 12:40; I Cor. 15:3-4*

Q. 28. Wherein consisteth Christ's exaltation?

A. Christ's exaltation consisteth in his rising again from the dead on the third day,[79] in ascending up into heaven,[80] in sitting at the right hand[81] of God the Father, and in coming to judge the world at the last day.[82]

[79]. *I Cor. 15:4*
[80]. *Ps. 68:18; Acts 1:11; Eph. 4:8*
[81]. *Ps. 110:1; Acts 2:33-34; Heb. 1:3*
[82]. *Matt. 16:27; Acts 17:31*

Q. 29. How are we made partakers of the redemption purchased by Christ?

A. We are made partakers of the redemption purchased by Christ, by the effectual application of it to us by his Holy Spirit.[83]

[83]. *Titus 3:4-7*

Q. 30. How doth the Spirit apply to us the redemption purchased by Christ?

A. The Spirit applieth to us the redemption purchased by Christ, by working faith in us,[84] and thereby uniting us to Christ in our effectual calling.[85]

[84]. Rom. 10:17; ICor. 2:12-16; Eph. 2:8; Phil. 1:29
[85]. John 15:5; ICor. 1:9; Eph. 3:17

Q. 31. What is effectual calling?

A. Effectual calling is the work of God's Spirit, whereby, convincing us of our sin and misery, enlightening our minds in the knowledge of Christ,[86] and renewing our wills,[87] he doth persuade and enable us to embrace Jesus Christ,[88] freely offered to us in the gospel.[89]

[86]. Acts 26:18; ICor. 2:10, 12; II Cor. 4:6; Eph. 1:17-18
[87]. Deut. 30:6; Ezk. 36:26-27; John 3:5; Titus 3:5
[88]. John 6:44-45; Acts 16:14
[89]. Isa. 45:22; Matt. 11:28-30; Rev. 22:17

Q. 32. What benefits do they that are effectually called partake of in this life?

A. They that are effectually called do in this life partake of justification, adoption, and sanctification, and the several benefits which in this life do either accompany or flow from them.[90]

[90]. Rom. 8:30; ICor. 1:30; 6:11; Eph. 1:5

Q. 33. What is justification?

A. Justification is an act of God's free grace,[91] wherein he pardoneth all our sins,[92] and accepteth us as righteous in His sight,[93] only for the righteousness of Christ imputed to us,[94] and received by faith alone.[95]

[91]. Rom. 3:24
[92]. Rom. 4:6-8; IICor. 5:19
[93]. IICor. 5:21

[94]. Rom. 4:6, 11; 5:19
[95]. Gal. 2:16; Phil. 3:9

Q. 34. What is adoption?

A. Adoption is an act of God's free grace,[96] a whereby we are received into the number, and have a right to all the privileges, of the sons of God.

[96]. I John 3:1; John 1:12; Rom. 8:17

Q. 35. What is sanctification?

A. Sanctification is the work of God's free grace,[97] whereby we are renewed in the whole man after the image of God,[98] and are enabled more and more to die unto sin, and live unto righteousness.[99]

[97]. Ezk. 36:27; Phil. 2:13; II Thess. 2:13
[98]. II Cor. 5:17; Eph. 4:23-24; I Thess. 5:23
[99]. Ezek. 36:25-27; Rom. 6:4, 6, 12-14; II Cor. 7:1; IPet. 2:24

Q. 36. What are the benefits which in this life do accompany or flow from justification, adoption, and sanctification?

A. The benefits which in this life do accompany or flow from justification, adoption, and sanctification, are, assurance of God's love,[100] peace of conscience,[101] joy in the Holy Ghost,[102] increase of grace,[103] and perseverance therein to the end.[104]

[100]. Rom. 5:5
[101]. Rom. 5:1
[102]. Rom. 14:17
[103]. II Pet. 3:18
[104]. Phil. 1:6; I Pet. 1:5

Q. 37. What benefits do believers receive from Christ at death?

A. The souls of believers are at their death made perfect in holiness,[105] and do immediately pass into glory;[106] and their bodies,

Adoniram Byfield or Bifield (d. 1660) was an English clergyman, one of the scribes to the Westminster Assembly. The surviving minutes of the Assembly, which according to a project to have them published "arguably constitute the most important unpublished religious text of seventeenth-century Britain", run to over half a million words and are almost all in Byfield's writing being still united to Christ,[107] do rest in their graves, till the resurrection.[108]

[105]. Heb. 12:23
[106]. Luke 23:43; II Cor. 5:6, 8; Phil. 1:23
[107]. I Thess. 4:14
[108]. Dan. 12:2; John 5:28-29; Acts 24:15

Q. 38. What benefits do believers receive from Christ at the resurrection?

A. At the resurrection, believers, being raised up in glory,[109] shall be openly acknowledged and acquitted in the day of judgment,[110] and made perfectly blessed in the full enjoying of God[111] to all eternity.[112]

[109]. Heb. 12:23
[110]. Luke 23:43; II Cor. 5:6, 8; Phil. 1:23
[111]. I Thess. 4:14
[112]. Dan. 12:2; John 5:28-29; Acts 24:15

Q. 39. What is the duty which God requireth of man?

A. The duty which God requireth of man, is obedience to his revealed will.[113]

[113]. Deut. 29:29; Mic. 6:8; I John 5:2-3

Q. 40. What did God at first reveal to man for the rule of his obedience?

A. The rule which God at first revealed to man for his obedience, was the moral law.[114]

[114]. Rom. 2:14-15; 10:5

Q. 41. Wherein is the moral law summarily comprehended?

A. The moral law is summarily comprehended in the ten commandments.[115]

[115]. Deut. 4:13; Matt. 19:17-19

Q. 42. What is the sum of the ten commandments?

A. The sum of the ten commandments is, to love the Lord our God with all our heart, with all our soul, with all our strength, and with all our mind; and our neighbor as ourselves.[116]
[116]. Matt. 22:37-40

Q. 43. What is the preface to the ten commandments?

A. The preface to the ten commandments is in these words, I am the Lord thy God, which have brought thee out of the land of Egypt, out of the house of bondage.[117]
[117]. Ex. 20:2; Deut. 5:6

Q. 44. What doth the preface to the ten commandments teach us?

A. The preface to the ten commandments teacheth us, that because God is the Lord, and our God, and Redeemer, therefore we are bound to keep all his commandments.[118]
[118]. Luke 1:74-75; I Pet. 1:14-19

Q. 45. Which is the first commandment?

A. The first commandment is, Thou shalt have no other gods before me.[119]
[119]. Ex. 20:3; Deut. 5:7

Q. 46. What is required in the first commandment?

A. The first commandment requireth us to know and acknowledge God to be the only true God, and our God; and to worship and glorify him accordingly.[120]
[120]. I Chron. 28:9; Isa. 45:20-25; Matt. 4:10

Q. 47. What is forbidden in the first commandment?

A. The first commandment forbiddeth the denying,[121] or not worshiping and glorifying, the true God as God,[122] and our God;[123]

and the giving of that worship and glory to any other, which is due to him alone.[124]

[121]. *Ps. 14:1*
[122]. *Rom. 1:20-21*
[123]. *Ps. 81:10-11*
[124]. *Ezek. 8:16-18; Rom. 1:25*

Q. 48. What are we specially taught by these words before me in the first commandment?

A. These words before me in the first commandment teach us, that God, who seeth all things, taketh notice of, and is much displeased with, the sin of having any other God.[125]

[125]. *Deut. 30:17-18; Ps. 44:20-21; Ezek. 8:12*

Q. 49. Which is the second commandment?

A. Thou shalt not make unto thee any graven image, or any likeness of any thing that is in heaven above, or that is in the earth beneath, or that is in the water under the earth: Thou shalt not bow down thyself to them, nor serve them: for I the LORD thy God am a jealous God, visiting the iniquity of the fathers upon the children unto the third and fourth generation of them that hate me; And shewing mercy unto thousands of them that love me, and keep my commandments.[126]

[126]. *Ex. 20:4-6; Deut. 5:8-10*

Q. 50. What is required in the second commandment?

A. The second commandment requireth the receiving, observing, and keeping pure and entire, all such religious worship and ordinances as God hath appointed in his Word.[127]

[127]. *Deut. 12:32; Matt. 28:20*

Q. 51. What is forbidden in the second commandment?

A. The second commandment forbiddeth the worshiping of God by

Joseph Caryl was born in London, educated at Merchant Taylors' School, and graduated at Exeter College, Oxford, and became preacher at Lincoln's Inn. He frequently preached before the Long Parliament, and was a member of the Westminster Assembly in 1643. By order of the parliament he attended Charles I in Holmby House, and in 1650 he was sent with John Owen to accompany Cromwell to Scotland. In 1662, following the Restoration, he was ejected from his church of St. Magnus near London Bridge. He continued, however, to minister to an Independent congregation in London till his death in March 1673, when John Owen succeeded him.

images,[128] or any other way not appointed in his Word.[129]

[128]. *Deut. 4:15-19; Rom. 1:22-23*
[129]. *Lev. 10:1-2; Jer. 19:4-5; Col. 2:18-23*

Q. 52. What are the reasons annexed to the second commandment?

A. The reasons annexed to the second commandment are, God's sovereignty over us,[130] his propriety in us,[131] and the zeal he hath to his own worship.[132]

[130]. *Ps. 95:2-3, 6-7; 96:9-10*
[131]. *Ex. 19:5; Ps. 45:11; Isa. 54:5*
[132]. *Ex. 34:14; ICor. 10:22*

Q. 53. Which is the third commandment?

A. The third commandment is, [133] Thou shalt not take the name of the Lord thy God in vain: for the Lord will not hold him guiltless that taketh his name in vain.

[133]. *Ex. 20:7; Deut. 5:11*

Q. 54. What is required in the third commandment?

A. The third commandment requireth the holy and reverent use of God's names, titles,[134] attributes,[135] ordinances,[136] Word,[137] and works.[138]

[134]. *Deut. 10:20; Ps. 29:2; Matt. 6:9*
[135]. *I Chron. 29:10-13; Rev. 15:3-4*
[136]. *Acts 2:42; I Cor. 11:27-28*
[137]. *Ps. 138:2; Rev. 22:18-19*
[138]. *Ps. 107:21-22; Rev. 4:11*

Q. 55. What is forbidden in the third commandment?

A. The third commandment forbiddeth all profaning or abusing of anything whereby God maketh himself known.[139]

[139]. *Lev. 19:12; Matt. 5:33-37; Jas. 5:12*

Q. 56. What is the reason annexed to the third commandment?

A. The reason annexed to the third commandment is, that however the breakers of this commandment may escape punishment from men, yet the Lord our God will not suffer them to escape his righteous judgment.[140]

[140]. Deut. 28:58-59; ISam. 3:13; 4:11

Q. 57. Which is the fourth commandment?

A. The fourth commandment is, Remember the sabbath day to keep it holy. Six days shalt thou labor, and do all thy work: but the seventh day is the sabbath of the Lord thy God: in it thou shalt not do any work, thou, nor thy son, nor thy daughter, thy manservant, nor thy maidservant, nor thy cattle, nor thy stranger that is within thy gates: For in six days the Lord made heaven and earth, the sea, and all that in them is, and rested the seventh day: wherefore the Lord blessed the sabbath day, and hallowed it.[141]

[141]. Ex. 20:8-11; Deut. 5:12-15

Q. 58. What is required in the fourth commandment?

A. The fourth commandment requireth the keeping holy to God such set times as he hath appointed in his Word; expressly one whole day in seven, to be a holy sabbath to himself.[142]

[142]. Ex. 31:13, 16-17

Q. 59. Which day of the seven hath God appointed to be the weekly sabbath?

A. From the beginning of the world to the resurrection of Christ, God appointed the seventh day of the week to be the weekly sabbath;[143] and the first day of the week ever since, to continue to the end of the world, which is the Christian sabbath.[144]

[143]. Gen. 2:2-3; Ex. 20:11
[144]. Mark 2:27-28; Acts 20:7; ICor. 16:2; Rev. 1:10

Q. 60. How is the sabbath to be sanctified?

A. The sabbath is to be sanctified by a holy resting all that day, even from such worldly employments and recreations as are lawful on other days;[145] and spending the whole time in the public and private exercises of God's worship,[146] except so much as is to be taken up in the works of necessity and mercy.[147]

[145]. Ex. 20:10; Neh. 13:15-22; Isa. 58:13-14
[146]. Ex. 20:8; Lev. 23:3; Luke 4:16; Acts 20:7
[147]. Matt. 12:1-13

Q. 61. What is forbidden in the fourth commandment?

A. The fourth commandment forbiddeth the omission, or careless performance, of the duties required, and the profaning the day by idleness, or doing that which is in itself sinful, or by unnecessary thoughts, words, or works, about our worldly employments or recreations.[148]

[148]. Neh. 13:15-22; Isa. 58:13-14; Amos 8:4-6

Q. 62. What are the reasons annexed to the fourth commandment?

A. The reasons annexed to the fourth commandment are, God's allowing us six days of the week for our own employments,[149] his challenging a special propriety in the seventh, his own example, and his blessing the sabbath day.[150]

[149]. Ex. 20:9; 31:15; Lev. 23:3
[150]. Gen. 2:2-3; Ex. 20:11; 31:17

Q. 63. Which is the fifth commandment?

A. The fifth commandment is, Honor thy father and thy mother: that thy days may be long upon the land which the Lord thy God giveth thee.[151]

[151]. Ex. 20:12; Deut. 5:16

Samuel Bolton (1606 – 1654) was an English clergyman, scholar, and Master of Christ's College, Cambridge. In 1643 he was chosen one of the Westminster assembly of divines. He was successively minister of St. Martin's, Ludgate Street, of St. Saviour's, Southwark, and of St. Andrew's, Holborn.

Q. 64. What is required in the fifth commandment?

A. The fifth commandment requireth the preserving the honor, and performing the duties, belonging to everyone in their several places and relations, as superiors, inferiors, or equals.[152]

[152]. Rom. 13:1, 7; Eph. 5:21-22, 24; 6:1, 4-5, 9; I Pet. 2:17

Q. 65. What is forbidden in the fifth commandment?

A. The fifth commandment forbiddeth the neglecting of, or doing anything against, the honor and duty which belongeth to everyone in their several places and relations.[153]

[153]. Matt. 15:4-6; Rom. 13:8

Q. 66. What is the reason annexed to the fifth commandment?

A. The reason annexed to the fifth commandment is, a promise of long life and prosperity (as far as it shall serve for God's glory and their own good) to all such as keep this commandment.[154]

[154]. Ex. 20:12; Deut. 5:16; Eph. 6:2-3

Q. 67. Which is the sixth commandment?

A. The sixth commandment is, Thou shalt not kill.[155]

[155]. Ex. 20:13; Deut. 5:17

Q. 68. What is required in the sixth commandment?

A. The sixth commandment requireth all lawful endeavors to preserve our own life, and the life of others.[156]

[156]. Eph. 5:28-29

Q. 69. What is forbidden in the sixth commandment?

A. The sixth commandment forbiddeth the taking away of our own life, or the life of our neighbor, unjustly, or whatsoever tendeth thereunto.[157]

[157]. Gen. 9:6; Matt. 5:22; I John 3:15

Q. 70. Which is the seventh commandment?

A. The seventh commandment is, Thou shalt not commit adultery.[158]

[158]. Ex. 20:14; Deut. 5:18

Q. 71. What is required in the seventh commandment?

A. The seventh commandment requireth the preservation of our own and our neighbor's chastity, in heart, speech, and behavior.[159]

[159]. I Cor. 7:2-3, 5; I Thess. 4:3-5

Q. 72. What is forbidden in the seventh commandment?

A. The seventh commandment forbiddeth all unchaste thoughts, words, and actions.[160]

[160]. Matt. 5:28; Eph. 5:3-4

Q. 73. Which is the eighth commandment?

A. The eighth commandment is, Thou shalt not steal.[161]

[161]. Ex. 20:15; Deut. 5:19

Q. 74. What is required in the eighth commandment?

A. The eighth commandment requireth the lawful procuring and furthering the wealth and outward estate of ourselves and others.[162]

[162]. Lev. 25:35; Eph. 4:28b; Phil. 2:4

Q. 75. What is forbidden in the eighth commandment?

A. The eighth commandment forbiddeth whatsoever doth, or may, unjustly hinder our own, or our neighbor's wealth or outward estate.[163]

[163]. Prov. 28:19ff; Eph. 4:28a; II Thess. 3:10; I Tim. 5:8

Q. 76. Which is the ninth commandment?

A. The ninth commandment is, Thou shalt not bear false witness against thy neighbor.[164]

[164]. Ex. 20:16; Deut. 5:20

Q. 77. What is required in the ninth commandment?

A. The ninth commandment requireth the maintaining and promoting of truth between man and man, and of our own and our neighbor's good name,[165] especially in witness-bearing.[166]

[165]. Zech. 8:16; Acts 25:10; III John 12
[166]. Prov. 14:5, 25

Q. 78. What is forbidden in the ninth commandment?

A. The ninth commandment forbiddeth whatsoever is prejudicial to truth, or injurious to our own, or our neighbor's, good name.[167]

[167]. Lev. 19:16; Ps. 15:3; Prov. 6:16-19; Luke 3:14

Q. 79. Which is the tenth commandment?

A. The tenth commandment is, Thou shalt not covet thy neighbor's house, thou shalt not covet thy neighbor's wife, nor his manservant, nor his maidservant, nor his ox, nor his ass, nor anything that is thy neighbor's.[168]

[168]. Ex. 20:17; Deut. 5:21

Q. 80. What is required in the tenth commandment?

A. The tenth commandment requireth full contentment with our own condition,[169] with a right and charitable frame of spirit toward our neighbor, and all that is his.[170]

[169]. Ps. 34:1; Phil. 4:11; ITim. 6:6; Heb. 13:5
[170]. Luke 15:6, 9, 11-32; Rom. 12:15; Phil. 2:4

Thomas Case (1598–1682) was an English clergyman of Presbyterian beliefs and a member of the Westminster Assembly, where he was one of the strongest advocates of theocracy, and a sympathizer with the Restoration of the Stuart monarchy. He was arrested on 2 May 1651, accused of being privy to the presbyterian plot to recall Charles II and spent about six months in the Tower of London. Later on he was deputed by presbyterians to congratulate Charles II at the Hague, 1660, at the time of the Restoration, and became chaplain to the king. He took part in the Savoy conference 1661, but was ejected for nonconformity at the time of the Act of Uniformity 1662.

Q. 81. What is forbidden in the tenth commandment?

A. The tenth commandment forbiddeth all discontentment with our own estate,[171] envying or grieving at the good of our neighbor, and all inordinate motions and affections to anything that is his.[172]

[171]. I Cor. 10:10; Jas. 3:14-16
[172]. Gal. 5:26; Col. 3:5

Q. 82. Is any man able perfectly to keep the commandments of God?

A. No mere man, since the fall, is able in this life perfectly to keep the commandments of God, but doth daily break them in thought, word, and deed.[173]

[173]. Gen. 8:21; Rom. 3:9ff, 23

Q. 83. Are all transgressions of the law equally heinous?

A. Some sins in themselves, and by reason of several aggravations, are more heinous in the sight of God than others.[174]

[174]. Ezek. 8:6, 13, 15; Matt. 11:20-24; John 19:11

Q. 84. What doth every sin deserve?

A. Every sin deserveth God's wrath and curse, both in this life, and that which is to come.[175]

[175]. Matt. 25:41; Gal. 3:10; Eph. 5:6; Jas. 2:10

Q. 85. What doth God require of us, that we may escape his wrath and curse, due to us for sin?

A. To escape the wrath and curse of God, due to us for sin, God requireth of us faith in Jesus Christ, repentance unto life,[176] with the diligent use of all the outward means whereby Christ communicateth to us the benefits of redemption.[177]

[176]. Mark 1:15; Acts 20:21
[177]: Acts 2:38; I Cor. 11:24-25; Col. 3:16

Q. 86. What is faith in Jesus Christ?

A. Faith in Jesus Christ is a saving grace,[178] whereby we receive and rest upon him alone for salvation, as he is offered to us in the gospel.[179]

[178]. Eph. 2:8-9; cf. Rom. 4:16
[179]. John 20:30-31; Gal. 2:15-16; Phil. 3:3-11

Q. 87. What is repentance unto life?

A. Repentance unto life is a saving grace,[180] whereby a sinner, out of a true sense of his sin, and apprehension of the mercy of God in Christ,[181] doth, with grief and hatred of his sin, turn from it unto God,[182] with full purpose of, and endeavor after, new obedience.[183]

[180]. Acts 11:18; II Tim. 2:25
[181]. Ps. 51:1-4; Joel 2:13; Luke 15:7, 10; Acts 2:37
[182]. Jer. 31:18-19; Luke 1:16-17; I Thess. 1:9
[183]. II Chron. 7:14; Ps. 119:57-64; Matt. 3:8; II Cor. 7:10

Q. 88. What are the outward and ordinary means whereby Christ communicateth to us the benefits of redemption?

A. The outward and ordinary means whereby Christ communicateth to us the benefits of redemption are, his ordinances, especially the Word, sacraments, and prayer; all which are made effectual to the elect for salvation.[184]

[184]. Matt. 28:18-20; Acts 21:41, 42

Q. 89. How is the Word made effectual to salvation?

A. The Spirit of God maketh the reading, but especially the preaching, of the Word, an effectual means of convincing and converting sinners, and of building them up in holiness and comfort, through faith, unto salvation.[185]

[185]. Neh. 8:8-9; Acts 20:32; Rom. 10:14-17; II Tim. 3:15-17

Q. 90. How is the Word to be read and heard, that it may become effectual to salvation?

A. That the Word may become effectual to salvation, we must attend thereunto with diligence, preparation, and prayer;[186] receive it with faith and love, lay it up in our hearts, and practice it in our lives.[187]

[186]. *Deut. 6:6ff; Ps. 119:18; I Pet. 2:1-2*
[187]. *Ps. 119:11; II Thess. 2:10; Heb. 4:2; Jas. 1:22-25*

Q. 91. How do the sacraments become effectual means of salvation?

A. The sacraments become effectual means of salvation, not from any virtue in them, or in him that doth administer them; but only by the blessing of Christ, and the working of his Spirit in them that by faith receive them.[188]

[188]. *I Cor. 3:7; cf. I Cor. 1:12-17*

Q. 92. What is a sacrament?

A. A sacrament is a holy ordinance instituted by Christ;[189] wherein, by sensible signs, Christ, and the benefits of the new covenant, are represented, sealed, and applied to believers.[190]

[189]. *Matt. 28:19; 26:26-28; Mark 14:22-25; Luke 22:19-20; I Cor. 1:22-26*
[190]. *Gal. 3:27; I Cor. 10:16-17*

Q. 93. Which are the sacraments of the New Testament?

A. The sacraments of the New Testament are, baptism,[191] and the Lord's Supper.[192]

[191] *Matt. 28:19*
[192] *1 Cor 11:23-26*

Thomas Baylie (1582–1663) was an English clergyman, member of the Westminster Assembly and Fifth Monarchist. He was elected demy of Magdalen College in 1600, and perpetual fellow of the college in 1611, being then M. A. Afterwards he became rector of Manningford Bruce, Wiltshirey, and he proceeded to the degree of B.D. in 1621, at which time he was a zealous puritan. On being turned out of his living after the Restoration, he set up a conventicle at Marlborough, Wiltshire. There he died and was buried in the church of St. Peter on 27 March 1663.

Q. 94. What is baptism?

A. Baptism is a sacrament, wherein the washing with water in the name of the Father, and of the Son, and of the Holy Ghost,[193] doth signify and seal our ingrafting into Christ, and partaking of the benefits of the covenant of grace, and our engagement to be the Lord's.[194]

[193] Matt 28:19
[194] Acts 2:38-42; 22:16; Rom 6:3-4; Gal3:26-27; 1 Pet 3:21

Q. 95. To whom is Baptism to be administered?

A. Baptism is not to be administered to any that are out of the visible church, till they profess their faith in Christ, and obedience to him;[195] but the infants of such as are members of the visible church are to be baptized.[196]

[195] Acts 2:41; 8:12, 36, 38; 18:8
[196] Gen 17:7, 9-11; Acts 2:38-39; 16:32-33; Col 2:11-12

Q. 96. What is the Lord's Supper?

A. The Lord's Supper is a sacrament, wherein, by giving and receiving bread and wine, according to Christ's appointment, his death is showed forth;[197] and the worthy receivers are, not after a corporal and carnal manner, but by faith, made partakers of his body and blood, with all his benefits, to their spiritual nourishment, and growth in grace.[198]

[197] Luke 22:19-20; 1 Cor 11:23-26
[198] 1 Cor 10:16-17

Q. 97. What is required for the worthy receiving of the Lord's Supper?

A. It is required of them that would worthily partake of the Lord's Supper, that they examine themselves of their knowledge to discern the Lord's body, of their faith to feed upon him, of their repentance, love, and new obedience; lest, coming unworthily, they eat and drink judgement to themselves.[199]

[199] 1 Cor 11:27-32

Q. 98. What is prayer?

A. Prayer is an offering up of our desires unto God,[200] for things agreeable to his will,[201] in the name of Christ,[202] with confession of our sins,[203] and thankful acknowledgement of his mercies.[204]

[200] Ps 10:17; 62:8; Matt 7:7-8
[201] 1 John 5:14
[202] John 16:23-24
[203] Ps 32:5-6; Dan 9:4-19; 1 John 1:9
[204] Ps 103:1-5; 136; Phil 4:6

Q. 99. What rule hath God given for our direction in prayer?

A. The whole Word of God is of use to direct us in prayer;[205] but the special rule of direction is that form of prayer which Christ taught his disciples, commonly called the Lord's Prayer.[206]

[205] 1 John 5:14
[206] Matt 6;9-13

Q. 100. What doth the preface of the Lord's Prayer teach us?

A. The preface of the Lord's Prayer, which is, Our Father which art in heaven, teacheth us to draw near to God with all holy reverence [207]and confidence,[208] as children to a father,[209] able and ready to help us;[210] and that we should pray with and for others.[211]

[207] Ps 95:6
[208] Eph 3:12
[209] Matt 7:9-11; Luke 11:11-13;Rom 8:15
[210] Eph 3:20
[211] Eph 6:18; 1 Tim 2:1-2

Q. 101. What do we pray for in the first petition?

A. In the first petition, which is, Hallowed be thy name, we pray that God would enable us, and others, to glorify him in all that whereby he maketh himself known;[212] and that he would dispose all things to his own glory.[213]

[212] Ps 67:1-3; 99:3; 100:3-4
[213] Rom 11:33-36; Rev 4:11

Q. 102. What do we pray for in the second petition?

A. In the second petition, which is, Thy kingdom come, we pray that Satan's kingdom may be destroyed;[214] and that the kingdom of grace may be advanced,[215] ourselves and others brought into it, and kept in it;[216] and that the kingdom of glory may be hastened.[217]

[214] Matt 12:25-28; Rom 16:20; 1 John 3:8
[215] Ps 72:8-11; Matt 24:14; 1 Cor 15:24-25
[216] Ps 119:5; Luke 22:32; 2 Thess 3:1-5
[217] Rev 22:20

Q. 103. What do we pray for in the third petition?

A. In the third petition, which is, Thy will be done in earth, as it is in heaven, we pray that God, by his grace, would make us able and willing to know, obey, and submit to his will in all things,[218] as the angels do in heaven.[219]

[218] Ps 19:14; 119; 1 Thess 5:23; Heb 13:20-21
[219] Ps 103:20-21; Heb 1:14

Q. 104. What do we pray for in the fourth petition?

A. In the fourth petition, which is, Give us this day our daily bread, we pray that of God's free gift we may receive a competent portion of the good things of this life, and enjoy his blessing with them.[220]

[220] Prov 30:8-9; Matt 6:31-34; Phil 4:11, 19; 1 Tim 6:6-8

Q. 105. What do we pray for in the fifth petition?

A. In the fifth petition, which is, And forgive us our debts, as we forgive our debtors, we pray that God, for Christ's sake, would freely pardon all our sins;[221] which we are the rather encouraged to ask, because by his grace we are enabled from the heart to forgive

others.[222]
[221] Ps 51:1-2, 7, 9; Dan 9:17-19; 1 John 1:7
[222] Matt 18:21-35; Eph 4:32; Col 3:13

Q. 106. What do we pray for in the sixth petition?

A. In the sixth petition, which is, And lead us not into temptation, but deliver us from evil, we pray that God would either keep us from being tempted to sin,[223] or support and deliver us when we are tempted.[224]

[223] Ps 19:13; Matt 26:41; John 17:15
[224] Luke 22:31-32; 1 Cor 10:13; 2 Cor 12;7-9; Heb 2:18

Q. 107. What doth the conclusion of the Lord's Prayer teach us?

A. The conclusion of the Lord's Prayer, which is, For thine is the kingdom, and the power, and the glory, forever. Amen, teacheth us to take our encouragement in prayer from God only,[225] and in our prayers to praise him, ascribing kingdom, power, and glory to him;[226] and, in testimony of our desire, and assurance to be heard, we say, Amen.[227]

[225] Dan 9:4, 7-9, 16-19; Luke 18:1,7-8
[226] 1 Chron 29:10-13; 1 Tim 1:17; Rev 5:11-13
[227] 1 Cor 14:16; Rev 22:20

Edmund Calamy (February 1600 – October 29, 1666) was an English Presbyterian church leader and divine. Known as "the elder", he was the first of four generations of nonconformist ministers bearing the same name.

Simeon Ashe (died 1662) was an English nonconformist clergyman, a member of the Westminster Assembly and chaplain to the Parliamentary leader Edward Montagu, 2nd Earl of Manchester. He began his career as minister in Staffordshire, but was ejected from his living on account of his refusal to read the Book of Sports and to conform to other ceremonies. On his dismissal Sir John Burgoyne befriended him and allowed him the use of an 'exempt' church at Wroxhall; and he was afterwards under the protection of Robert Greville, 2nd Baron Brooke.

Footnotes

[1] **Q1.** Psalm 86:9 All nations whom thou hast made shall come and worship before thee, O Lord; and shall glorify thy name.

Isaiah 60:21. Thy people also shall be all righteous: they shall inherit the land for ever, the branch of my planting, the work of my hands, that I may be glorified.

Romans 11:36. For of him, and through him, and to him, are all things: to whom be glory for ever. Amen.

1 Corinthians 6:20; 10:31. For ye are bought with a price: therefore glorify God in your body, and in your spirit, which are God's.... Whether therefore ye eat, or drink, or whatsoever ye do, do all to the glory of God.

Revelation 4:11. Thou art worthy, O Lord, to receive glory and honour and power: for thou hast created all things, and for thy pleasure they are and were created.

[2] Psalm 16:5-11. The LORD is the portion of mine inheritance and of my cup: thou maintainest my lot. The lines are fallen unto me in pleasant places; yea, I have a goodly heritage. I will bless the LORD, who hath given me counsel: my reins also instruct me in the night seasons. I have set the LORD always before me: because he is at my right hand, I shall not be moved. Therefore my heart is glad, and my glory rejoiceth: my flesh also shall rest in hope. For thou wilt not leave my soul in hell; neither wilt thou suffer thine Holy One to see corruption. Thou wilt show me the path of life: in thy presence is fulness of joy; at thy right hand there are pleasures for evermore.

Psalm 144:15. Happy is that people, that is in such a case: yea, happy is that people, whose God is the LORD.

Isaiah 12:2. Behold, God is my salvation; I will trust, and not be afraid: for the LORD JEHOVAH is my strength and my song; he also is become my salvation.

Luke 2:10. And the angel said unto them, Fear not: for, behold, I bring you good tidings of great joy, which shall be to all people.

Philippians 4:4. Rejoice in the Lord alway: and again I say, Rejoice.

Revelation 21:3-4. And I heard a great voice out of heaven saying, Behold, the tabernacle of God is with men, and he will dwell with them, and they shall be his people, and God himself shall be with them, and be their God. And God shall wipe away all tears from their eyes; and there shall be no more death, neither sorrow, nor crying, neither shall there be any more pain: for the former things are passed away.

Q2. Matthew 19:4-5. And he answered and said unto them, Have ye not read, that he which made them at the beginning made them male and female, And said, For this cause shall a man leave father and mother, and shall cleave to his wife: and they twain shall be one flesh?

With Genesis 2:24. Therefore shall a man leave his father and his mother, and shall cleave unto his wife: and they shall be one flesh.

Luke 24:27, 44. And beginning at Moses and all the prophets, he expounded unto them in all the scriptures the things concerning himself.... And he said unto them, These are the words which I spake unto you, while I was yet with you, that all things must be fulfilled, which were written in the law of Moses, and in the prophets, and in the psalms, concerning me.

1 Corinthians 2:13. Which things also we speak, not in the words which man's wisdom teacheth, but which the Holy Ghost teacheth; comparing spiritual things with spiritual.

1 Corinthians 14:37. If any man think himself to be a prophet, or spiritual, let him acknowledge that the things that I write unto you are the commandments of the Lord.

2 Peter 1:20-21. Knowing this first, that no prophecy of the scripture is of any private interpretation. For the prophecy came not in old time by the will of man: but holy men of God spake as they were moved by the Holy Ghost.

2 Peter 3:2, 15-16. That ye may be mindful of the words which were spoken before by the holy prophets, and of the commandment of us the apostles of the Lord and Saviour.... And account that the longsuffering of our Lord is salvation; even as our beloved brother Paul also according to the wisdom given unto him hath written unto you; As also in all his epistles, speaking in them of these things; in which are some things hard to be understood, which they that are unlearned and unstable wrest, as they do also the other scriptures, unto their own destruction.

[4] Deuteronomy 4:2. Ye shall not add unto the word which I command you, neither shall ye diminish ought from it, that ye may keep the commandments of the LORD your God which I command you.

Psalm 19:7-11. The law of the LORD is perfect, converting the soul: the testimony of the LORD is sure, making wise the simple. The statutes of the LORD are right, rejoicing the heart: the commandment of the LORD is pure, enlightening the eyes. The fear of the LORD is clean, enduring for ever: the judgments of the LORD are true and righteous altogether. More to be desired are they than gold, yea, than much fine gold: sweeter also than honey and the honeycomb. Moreover by them is thy servant warned: and in keeping of them there is great reward.

Isaiah 8:20. To the law and to the testimony: if they speak not according to this word, it is because there is no light in them.

John 15:11. These things have I spoken unto you, that my joy might remain in you, and that your joy might be full.

John 20:30-31. And many other signs truly did Jesus in the presence of his disciples, which are not written in this book: But these are written, that ye might believe that Jesus is the Christ, the Son of God; and that believing ye might have life through his name.

Acts 17:11. These were more noble than those in Thessalonica, in that they received the word with all readiness of mind, and searched the scriptures daily, whether those things were so.

2 Timothy 3:15-17. And that from a child thou hast known the holy scriptures, which are able to make thee wise unto salvation through faith which is in Christ Jesus. All scripture is given by inspiration of God, and is profitable for doctrine, for reproof, for correction, for instruction in righteousness: That the man of God may be perfect, thoroughly furnished unto all good works. 1

John 1:4. And these things write we unto you, that your joy may be full.

Q3. Genesis 1:1. In the beginning God created the heaven and the earth.

John 5:39. Search the scriptures; for in them ye think ye have eternal life: and they are they which testify of me.

John 20:31. But these are written, that ye might believe that Jesus is the Christ, the Son of God; and that believing ye might have life through his name.

Romans 10:17. So then faith cometh by hearing, and hearing by the word of God.

2 Timothy 3:15. And that from a child thou hast known the holy scriptures, which are able to make thee wise unto salvation through faith which is in Christ Jesus.

Deuteronomy 10:12-13. And now, Israel, what doth the LORD thy God require of thee, but to fear the LORD thy God, to walk in all his ways, and to love him, and to serve the LORD thy God with all thy heart and with all thy soul, To keep the commandments of the LORD, and his statutes, which I command thee this day for thy good?

Joshua 1:8. This book of the law shall not depart out of thy mouth; but thou shalt meditate therein day and night, that thou mayest observe to do according to all that is written therein: for then thou shalt make thy way prosperous, and then thou shalt have good success.

Psalm 119:105. Thy word is a lamp unto my feet, and a light unto my path.

Micah 6:8. He hath showed thee, O man, what is good; and what doth the LORD require of thee, but to do justly, and to love mercy, and to walk humbly with thy God?

2 Timothy 3:16-17. All scripture is given by inspiration of God, and is profitable for doctrine, for reproof, for correction, for instruction in righteousness: That the man of God may be perfect, thoroughly furnished unto all good works.

Q4. Deuteronomy 4:15-19. Take ye therefore good heed unto yourselves; for ye saw no manner of similitude on the day that the LORD spake unto you in Horeb out of the midst of the fire: Lest ye corrupt yourselves, and make you a graven image, the similitude of any figure, the likeness of male or female, The likeness of any beast that is on the earth, the likeness of any winged fowl that flieth in the air, The likeness of any thing that creepeth on the ground, the likeness of any fish that is in the waters beneath the earth: And lest thou lift up thine eyes unto heaven, and when thou seest the sun, and the moon, and the stars, even all the host of heaven, shouldest be driven to worship them, and serve them, which the LORD thy God hath divided unto all nations under the whole heaven.

Luke 24:39. Behold my hands and my feet, that it is I myself: handle me, and see; for a spirit hath not flesh and bones, as ye see me have. John 1:18. No man hath seen God at any time; the only begotten Son, which is in the bosom of the Father, he hath declared him.

John 4:24. God is a Spirit: and they that worship him must worship him in spirit and in truth.

Acts 17:29. Forasmuch then as we are the offspring of God, we ought not to think that the Godhead is like unto gold, or silver, or stone, graven by art and man's device.

1 Kings 8:27. But will God indeed dwell on the earth? behold, the heaven and heaven of heavens cannot contain thee; how much less this house that I have builded?

Psalm 139:7-10. Whither shall I go from thy spirit? or whither shall I flee from thy presence? If I ascend up into heaven, thou art there: if I make my bed in hell, behold, thou art there. If I take the wings of the morning, and dwell in the uttermost parts of the sea; Even there shall thy hand lead me, and thy right hand shall hold me.

Psalm 145:3. Great is the LORD, and greatly to be praised; and his greatness is unsearchable.

Psalm 147:5. Great is our Lord, and of great power: his understanding is infinite.

Jeremiah 23:24. Can any hide himself in secret places that I shall not see him? saith the LORD. Do not I fill heaven and earth? saith the LORD.

Romans 11:33-36. O the depth of the riches both of the wisdom and knowledge of God! how unsearchable are his judgments, and his ways past finding out! For who hath known the mind of the Lord? or who hath been his counsellor? Or who hath first given to him, and it shall be recompensed unto him again? For of him, and through him, and to him, are all things: to whom be glory for ever. Amen.

Deuteronomy 33:27. The eternal God is thy refuge, and underneath are the everlasting arms: and he shall thrust out the enemy from before thee; and shall say, Destroy them.

Psalm 90:2. Before the mountains were brought forth, or ever thou hadst formed the earth and the world, even from everlasting to everlasting, thou art God.

Psalm 102:12, 24-27. But thou, O LORD, shalt endure for ever; and thy remembrance unto all generations.... I said, O my God, take me not away in the midst of my days: thy years are throughout all generations. Of old hast thou laid the foundation of the earth: and the heavens are the work of thy hands. They shall perish, but thou shalt endure: yea, all of them shall wax old like a garment; as a vesture shalt thou change them, and they shall be changed: But thou art the same, and thy years shall have no end.

Revelation 1:4, 8. John to the seven churches which are in Asia: Grace be unto you, and peace, from him which is, and which was, and which is to come; and from the seven Spirits which are before his throne.... I am Alpha and Omega, the beginning and the ending, saith the Lord, which is, and which was, and which is to come, the Almighty.

[10] Psalm 33:11. The counsel of the LORD standeth for ever, the thoughts of his heart to all generations.

Malachi 3:6. For I am the LORD, I change not; therefore ye sons of Jacob are not consumed.

Hebrews 1:12. And as a vesture shalt thou fold them up, and they shall be changed: but thou art the same, and thy years shall not fail.

Hebrews 6:17-18. Wherein God, willing more abundantly to show unto the heirs of promise the immutability of his counsel, confirmed it by an oath: That by two immutable things, in which it was impossible for God to lie, we might have a strong consolation, who have fled for refuge to lay hold upon the hope set before us: Hebrews 13:8. Jesus Christ the same yesterday, and to day, and for ever.

James 1:17. Every good gift and every perfect gift is from above, and cometh down from the Father of lights, with whom is no variableness, neither shadow of turning.

[11] Exodus 3:14. And God said unto Moses, I AM THAT I AM: and he said, Thus shalt thou say unto the children of Israel, I AM hath sent me unto you.

Psalm 115:2-3. Wherefore should the heathen say, Where is now their God? But our God is in the heavens: he hath done whatsoever he hath pleased.

1 Timothy 1:17. Now unto the King eternal, immortal, invisible, the only wise God, be honour and glory for ever and ever. Amen.

1 Timothy 6:15-16. Which in his times he shall show, who is the blessed and only Potentate, the King of kings, and Lord of lords; Who only hath immortality, dwelling in the light which no man can approach unto; whom no man hath seen, nor can see: to whom be honour and power everlasting. Amen.

Psalm 104:24. O LORD, how manifold are thy works! in wisdom hast thou made them all: the earth is full of thy riches.

Romans 11:33-34. O the depth of the riches both of the wisdom and knowledge of God! how unsearchable are his judgments, and his ways past finding out! For who hath known the mind of the Lord? or who hath been his counsellor?

Hebrews 4:13. Neither is there any creature that is not manifest in his sight: but all things are naked and opened unto the eyes of him with whom we have to do.

1 John 3:20. For if our heart condemn us, God is greater than our heart, and knoweth all things.

Genesis 17:1. And when Abram was ninety years old and nine, the LORD appeared to Abram, and said unto him, I am the Almighty God; walk before me, and be thou perfect.

Psalm 62:11. God hath spoken once; twice have I heard this; that power belongeth unto God.

Jeremiah 32:17. Ah Lord GOD! behold, thou hast made the heaven and the earth by thy great power and stretched out arm, and there is nothing too hard for thee:

Matthew 19:26. But Jesus beheld them, and said unto them, With men this is impossible; but with God all things are possible.

Revelation 1:8. I am Alpha and Omega, the beginning and the ending, saith the Lord, which is, and which was, and which is to come, the Almighty.

¹⁴   Hebrews 1:13. But to which of the angels said he at any time, Sit on my right hand, until I make thine enemies thy footstool?

1 Peter 1:15-16. But as he which hath called you is holy, so be ye holy in all manner of conversation; Because it is written, Be ye holy; for I am holy.

1 John 3:3, 5. And every man that hath this hope in him purifieth himself, even as he is pure.... And ye know that he was manifested to take away our sins; and in him is no sin.

Revelation 15:4. Who shall not fear thee, O Lord, and glorify thy name? for thou only art holy: for all nations shall come and worship before thee; for thy judgments are made manifest.

¹⁵   Genesis 18:25. That be far from thee to do after this manner, to slay the righteous with the wicked: and that the righteous should be as the wicked, that be far from thee: Shall not the Judge of all the earth do right?

Exodus 34:6-7. And the LORD passed by before him, and proclaimed, The LORD, The LORD God, merciful and gracious, longsuffering, and abundant in goodness and truth, Keeping mercy for thousands, forgiving iniquity and transgression and sin, and that will by no means clear the guilty; visiting the iniquity of the fathers upon the children, and upon the children's children, unto the third and to the fourth generation.

Deuteronomy 32:4. He is the Rock, his work is perfect: for all his ways are judgment: a God of truth and without iniquity, just and right is he.

Psalm 96:13. Before the LORD: for he cometh, for he cometh to judge the earth: he shall judge the world with righteousness, and the people with his truth.

Romans 3:5, 26. But if our unrighteousness commend the righteousness of God, what shall we say? Is God unrighteous who taketh vengeance? (I speak as a man).... To declare, I say, at this time his righteousness: that he might be just, and the justifier of him which believeth in Jesus.

[16]   Psalm 103:5. Who satisfieth thy mouth with good things; so that thy youth is renewed like the eagle's.

Psalm 107:8. Oh that men would praise the LORD for his goodness, and for his wonderful works to the children of men!

Matthew 19:7. They say unto him, Why did Moses then command to give a writing of divorcement, and to put her away?

Romans 2:4. Or despisest thou the riches of his goodness and forbearance and longsuffering; not knowing that the goodness of God leadeth thee to repentance?

[17]   Exodus 34:6. And the LORD passed by before him, and proclaimed, The LORD, The LORD God, merciful and gracious, longsuffering, and abundant in goodness and truth,

Deuteronomy 32:4. He is the Rock, his work is perfect: for all his ways are judgment: a God of truth and without iniquity, just and right is he.

Psalm 86:15. But thou, O Lord, art a God full of compassion, and gracious, longsuffering, and plenteous in mercy and truth.

Psalm 117:2. For his merciful kindness is great toward us: and the truth of the LORD endureth for ever. Praise ye the LORD.

Hebrews 6:18. That by two immutable things, in which it was impossible for God to lie, we might have a strong consolation, who have fled for refuge to lay hold upon the hope set before us.

[18]   **Q5**. Deuteronomy 6:4. Hear, O Israel: The LORD our God is one LORD:

Isaiah 44:6. Thus saith the LORD the King of Israel, and his redeemer the LORD of hosts; I am the first, and I am the last; and beside me there is no God.

Isaiah 45:21-22. Tell ye, and bring them near; yea, let them take counsel together: who hath declared this from ancient time? who hath told it from that time? have not I the LORD? and there is no God else beside me; a just God and a Saviour; there is none beside me. Look unto me, and be ye saved, all the ends of the earth: for I am God, and there is none else.

 1 Corinthians 8:4-6. As concerning therefore the eating of those things that are offered in sacrifice unto idols, we know that an idol is nothing in the world, and that there is none other God but one. For though there be that are called gods, whether in heaven or in earth, (as there be gods many, and lords many,) But to us there is but one God, the Father, of whom are all things, and we in him; and one Lord Jesus Christ, by whom are all things, and we by him.

 Jeremiah 10:10. But the LORD is the true God, he is the living God, and an everlasting king: at his wrath the earth shall tremble, and the nations shall not be able to abide his indignation.

 John 17:3. And this is life eternal, that they might know thee the only true God, and Jesus Christ, whom thou hast sent.

 1 Thessalonians 1:9. For they themselves show of us what manner of entering in we had unto you, and how ye turned to God from idols to serve the living and true God;

 1 John 5:20. And we know that the Son of God is come, and hath given us an understanding, that we may know him that is true, and we are in him that is true, even in his Son Jesus Christ. This is the true God, and eternal life.

 Q6. Matthew 3:16-17. And Jesus, when he was baptized, went up straightway out of the water: and, lo, the heavens were opened unto him, and he saw the Spirit of God descending like a dove, and lighting upon him: And lo a voice from heaven, saying, This is my beloved Son, in whom I am well pleased.

 Matthew 28:19. Go ye therefore, and teach all nations, baptizing them in the name of the Father, and of the Son, and of the Holy Ghost:

 2 Corinthians 13:14. The grace of the Lord Jesus Christ, and the love of God, and the communion of the Holy Ghost, be

with you all. Amen.

1 Peter 1:2. Elect according to the foreknowledge of God the Father, through sanctification of the Spirit, unto obedience and sprinkling of the blood of Jesus Christ: Grace unto you, and peace, be multiplied.

Psalm 45:6. Thy throne, O God, is for ever and ever: the sceptre of thy kingdom is a right sceptre. John 1:1. In the beginning was the Word, and the Word was with God, and the Word was God.

John 17:5. And now, O Father, glorify thou me with thine own self with the glory which I had with thee before the world was.

Acts 5:3-4. But Peter said, Ananias, why hath Satan filled thine heart to lie to the Holy Ghost, and to keep back part of the price of the land? Whiles it remained, was it not thine own? and after it was sold, was it not in thine own power? why hast thou conceived this thing in thine heart? thou hast not lied unto men, but unto God.

Romans 9:5. Whose are the fathers, and of whom as concerning the flesh Christ came, who is over all, God blessed for ever. Amen.

Colossians 2:9. For in him dwelleth all the fulness of the Godhead bodily.

Jude 1:24-25. Now unto him that is able to keep you from falling, and to present you faultless before the presence of his glory with exceeding joy, To the only wise God our Saviour, be glory and majesty, dominion and power, both now and for ever. Amen.

Q7. Psalm 33:11. The counsel of the LORD standeth for ever, the thoughts of his heart to all generations.

Isaiah 14:24. The LORD of hosts hath sworn, saying, Surely as I have thought, so shall it come to pass; and as I have purposed, so shall it stand:

Acts 2:23. Him, being delivered by the determinate counsel and foreknowledge of God, ye have taken, and by wicked hands have crucified and slain:

Ephesians 1:11-12. In whom also we have obtained an inheritance, being predestinated according to the purpose of him who worketh all things after the counsel of his own will: That we should be to the praise of his glory, who first trusted in Christ.

Q8. Psalm 148:8. Fire, and hail; snow, and vapours; stormy wind fulfilling his word:

Isaiah 40:26. Lift up your eyes on high, and behold who hath created these things, that bringeth out their host by number: he calleth them all by names by the greatness of his might, for that he is strong in power; not one faileth.

Daniel 4:35. And all the inhabitants of the earth are reputed as nothing: and he doeth according to his will in the army of heaven, and among the inhabitants of the earth: and none can stay his hand, or say unto him, What doest thou?

Acts 4:24-28. And when they heard that, they lifted up their voice to God with one accord, and said, Lord, thou art God, which hast made heaven, and earth, and the sea, and all that in them is: Who by the mouth of thy servant David hast said, Why did the heathen rage, and the people imagine vain things? The kings of the earth stood up, and the rulers were gathered together against the Lord, and against his Christ. For of a truth against thy holy child Jesus, whom thou hast anointed, both Herod, and Pontius Pilate, with the Gentiles, and the people of Israel, were gathered together, For to do whatsoever thy hand and thy counsel determined before to be done.

Revelation 4:11. Thou art worthy, O Lord, to receive glory and honour and power: for thou hast created all things, and for thy pleasure they are and were created.

Q9. Genesis 1:1. In the beginning God created the heaven and the earth.

Psalm 33:6, 9. By the word of the LORD were the heavens made; and all the host of them by the breath of his mouth.... For he spake, and it was done; he commanded, and it stood fast.

Hebrews 11:3. Through faith we understand that the worlds were framed by the word of God, so that things which are seen were not made of things which do appear.

Genesis 1:31. And God saw every thing that he had made, and, behold, it was very good. And the evening and the morning were the sixth day.

Q10. Genesis 1:27. So God created man in his own image, in the image of God created he him; male and female created he them.

Colossians 3:10. And have put on the new man, which is renewed in knowledge after the image of him that created him.

Ephesians 4:24. And that ye put on the new man, which after God is created in righteousness and true holiness.

Genesis 1:28. And God blessed them, and God said unto them, Be fruitful, and multiply, and replenish the earth, and subdue it: and have dominion over the fish of the sea, and over the fowl of the air, and over every living thing that moveth upon the earth.

Psalm 8. O LORD our Lord, how excellent is thy name in all the earth! who hast set thy glory above the heavens. Out of the mouth of babes and sucklings hast thou ordained strength because of thine enemies, that thou mightest still the enemy and the avenger. When I consider thy heavens, the work of thy fingers, the moon and the stars, which thou hast ordained; What is man, that thou art mindful of him? and the son of man, that thou visitest him? For thou hast made him a little lower than the angels, and hast crowned him with glory and honour. Thou madest him to have dominion over the works of thy hands; thou hast put all things under his feet: All sheep and oxen, yea, and the beasts of the field; The fowl of the air, and the fish of the sea, and whatsoever passeth through the paths of the seas. O LORD our Lord, how excellent is thy name in all the earth!

[30] **Q11**. Psalm 145:17. The LORD is righteous in all his ways, and holy in all his works.

[31] Psalm 104:24. O LORD, how manifold are thy works! in wisdom hast thou made them all: the earth is full of thy riches.

[32] Hebrews 1:3. Who being the brightness of his glory, and the express image of his person, and upholding all things by the word of his power, when he had by himself purged our sins, sat down on the right hand of the Majesty on high

[33] Nehemiah 9:6. Thou, even thou, art LORD alone; thou hast made heaven, the heaven of heavens, with all their host, the earth, and all things that are therein, the seas, and all that is therein, and thou preservest them all; and the host of heaven worshippeth thee.

[34] Ephesians 1:19-22. And what is the exceeding greatness of his power to us-ward who believe, according to the working of his mighty power, Which he wrought in Christ, when he raised him from the dead, and set him at his own right hand in the heavenly places, Far above all principality, and power, and might, and dominion, and every name that is named, not only in this world, but also in that which is to come: And hath put all things under his feet, and gave him to be the head over all things to the church

[35] Psalm 36:6. Thy righteousness is like the great mountains; thy judgments are a great deep: O LORD, thou preservest man and beast.

Proverbs 16:33. The lot is cast into the lap; but the whole disposing thereof is of the LORD.

Matthew 10:30. But the very hairs of your head are all numbered.

[36] **Q12**. Genesis 2:16-17. And the LORD God commanded

the man, saying, Of every tree of the garden thou mayest freely eat: But of the tree of the knowledge of good and evil, thou shalt not eat of it: for in the day that thou eatest thereof thou shalt surely die.

James 2:10. For whosoever shall keep the whole law, and yet offend in one point, he is guilty of all.

[37] **Q13**. Genesis 3:6-8, 13. And when the woman saw that the tree was good for food, and that it was pleasant to the eyes, and a tree to be desired to make one wise, she took of the fruit thereof, and did eat, and gave also unto her husband with her; and he did eat. And the eyes of them both were opened, and they knew that they were naked; and they sewed fig leaves together, and made themselves aprons. And they heard the voice of the LORD God walking in the garden in the cool of the day: and Adam and his wife hid themselves from the presence of the LORD God amongst the trees of the garden.... And the LORD God said unto the woman, What is this that thou hast done? And the woman said, The serpent beguiled me, and I did eat.

2 Corinthians 11:3. But I fear, lest by any means, as the serpent beguiled Eve through his subtlety, so your minds should be corrupted from the simplicity that is in Christ.

[38] **Q14**. Leviticus 5:17. And if a soul sin, and commit any of these things which are forbidden to be done by the commandments of the LORD; though he wist it not, yet is he guilty, and shall bear his iniquity.

James 4:17. Therefore to him that knoweth to do good, and doeth it not, to him it is sin.

1 John 3:4. Whosoever committeth sin transgresseth also the law: for sin is the transgression of the law.

[39] **Q15**. Genesis 3:6. And when the woman saw that the tree was good for food, and that it was pleasant to the eyes, and a tree to be desired to make one wise, she took of the fruit thereof, and did eat, and gave also unto her husband with her; and he did eat.

Q16. Genesis 2:16-17. And the LORD God commanded the man, saying, Of every tree of the garden thou mayest freely eat: But of the tree of the knowledge of good and evil, thou shalt not eat of it: for in the day that thou eatest thereof thou shalt surely die.

James 2:10. For whosoever shall keep the whole law, and yet offend in one point, he is guilty of all.

Romans 5:12-21. Wherefore, as by one man sin entered into the world, and death by sin; and so death passed upon all men, for that all have sinned: (For until the law sin was in the world: but sin is not imputed when there is no law. Nevertheless death reigned from Adam to Moses, even over them that had not sinned after the similitude of Adam's transgression, who is the figure of him that was to come. But not as the offence, so also is the free gift. For if through the offence of one many be dead, much more the grace of God, and the gift by grace, which is by one man, Jesus Christ, hath abounded unto many. And not as it was by one that sinned, so is the gift: for the judgment was by one to condemnation, but the free gift is of many offences unto justification. For if by one man's offence death reigned by one; much more they which receive abundance of grace and of the gift of righteousness shall reign in life by one, Jesus Christ.) Therefore as by the offence of one judgment came upon all men to condemnation; even so by the righteousness of one the free gift came upon all men unto justification of life. For as by one man's disobedience many were made sinners, so by the obedience of one shall many be made righteous. Moreover the law entered, that the offence might abound. But where sin abounded, grace did much more abound: That as sin hath reigned unto death, even so might grace reign through righteousness unto eternal life by Jesus Christ our Lord.

1 Corinthians 15:22. For as in Adam all die, even so in Christ shall all be made alive.

Q17. Genesis 3:16-19, 23. Unto the woman he said, I will greatly multiply thy sorrow and thy conception; in sorrow thou shalt bring forth children; and thy desire shall be to thy husband, and he shall rule over thee. And unto Adam he said, Because thou hast hearkened unto the voice of thy wife, and hast eaten of the tree, of which I commanded thee, saying, Thou shalt not eat of it: cursed is the ground for thy sake; in sorrow shalt thou eat of it all the days of thy life; Thorns also and thistles shall it bring forth to thee; and thou shalt eat the herb of the field; In the sweat of thy face shalt thou eat bread, till thou return unto the ground; for out of it wast thou taken: for dust thou art, and unto dust shalt thou return.... Therefore the LORD God sent him forth from the garden of Eden, to till the ground from whence he was taken.

Romans 3:16. Destruction and misery are in their ways:

Romans 5:12. Wherefore, as by one man sin entered into the world, and death by sin; and so death passed upon all men, for that all have sinned:

Ephesians 2:1. And you hath he quickened, who were dead in trespasses and sins.

Q18. Romans 5:12, 19. Wherefore, as by one man sin entered into the world, and death by sin; and so death passed upon all men, for that all have sinned.... For as by one man's disobedience many were made sinners, so by the obedience of one shall many be made righteous.

Romans 3:10. As it is written, There is none righteous, no, not one:

Colossians 3:10. And have put on the new man, which is renewed in knowledge after the image of him that created him:

Ephesians 4:24. And that ye put on the new man, which after God is created in righteousness and true holiness.

Psalm 51:5. Behold, I was shapen in iniquity, and in sin did my mother conceive me.

John 3:6. That which is born of the flesh is flesh; and that which is born of the Spirit is spirit.

Romans 3:18. There is no fear of God before their eyes.

Romans 8:7-8. Because the carnal mind is enmity against God: for it is not subject to the law of God, neither indeed can be. So then they that are in the flesh cannot please God.

Ephesians 2:3. Among whom also we all had our conversation in times past in the lusts of our flesh, fulfilling the desires of the flesh and of the mind; and were by nature the children of wrath, even as others.

Genesis 6:5. And God saw that the wickedness of man was great in the earth, and that every imagination of the thoughts of his heart was only evil continually.

Psalm 53:1-3. The fool hath said in his heart, There is no God. Corrupt are they, and have done abominable iniquity: there is none that doeth good. God looked down from heaven upon the children of men, to see if there were any that did understand, that did seek God. Every one of them is gone back: they are altogether become filthy; there is none that doeth good, no, not one.

Matthew 15:19. For out of the heart proceed evil thoughts, murders, adulteries, fornications, thefts, false witness, blasphemies:

Romans 3:10-18, 23. As it is written, There is none righteous, no, not one: There is none that understandeth, there is none that seeketh after God. They are all gone out of the way, they are together become unprofitable; there is none that doeth good, no, not one. Their throat is an open sepulchre; with their tongues they have used deceit; the poison of asps is under their lips: Whose mouth is full of cursing and bitterness: Their feet are swift to shed blood: Destruction and misery are in their ways: And the way of peace have they not known: There is no fear of God before their eyes.... For all have sinned, and come short of the glory of God;

Galatians 5:19-21. Now the works of the flesh are

manifest, which are these; Adultery, fornication, uncleanness, lasciviousness, Idolatry, witchcraft, hatred, variance, emulations, wrath, strife, seditions, heresies, Envyings, murders, drunkenness, revellings, and such like: of the which I tell you before, as I have also told you in time past, that they which do such things shall not inherit the kingdom of God.

James 1:14-15. But every man is tempted, when he is drawn away of his own lust, and enticed. Then when lust hath conceived, it bringeth forth sin: and sin, when it is finished, bringeth forth death.

Genesis 3:8, 24. And they heard the voice of the LORD God walking in the garden in the cool of the day: and Adam and his wife hid themselves from the presence of the LORD God amongst the trees of the garden.... So he drove out the man; and he placed at the east of the garden of Eden Cherubims, and a flaming sword which turned every way, to keep the way of the tree of life.

John 8:34, 42, 44. Jesus answered them, Verily, verily, I say unto you, Whosoever committeth sin is the servant of sin.... Jesus said unto them, If God were your Father, ye would love me: for I proceeded forth and came from God; neither came I of myself, but he sent me.... Ye are of your father the devil, and the lusts of your father ye will do. He was a murderer from the beginning, and abode not in the truth, because there is no truth in him. When he speaketh a lie, he speaketh of his own: for he is a liar, and the father of it.

Ephesians 2:12. That at that time ye were without Christ, being aliens from the commonwealth of Israel, and strangers from the covenants of promise, having no hope, and without God in the world:

Ephesians 4:18. Having the understanding darkened, being alienated from the life of God through the ignorance that is in them, because of the blindness of their heart.

Q19. John 3:36. He that believeth on the Son hath everlasting life: and he that believeth not the Son shall not see life; but the wrath of God abideth on him.

Romans 1:18. For the wrath of God is revealed from heaven against all ungodliness and unrighteousness of men, who hold the truth in unrighteousness;

Ephesians 2:3. Among whom also we all had our conversation in times past in the lusts of our flesh, fulfilling the desires of the flesh and of the mind; and were by nature the children of wrath, even as others.

Ephesians 5:6. Let no man deceive you with vain words: for because of these things cometh the wrath of God upon the children of disobedience.

Galatians 3:10. For as many as are of the works of the law are under the curse: for it is written, Cursed is every one that continueth not in all things which are written in the book of the law to do them.

Revelation 22:3. And there shall be no more curse: but the throne of God and of the Lamb shall be in it; and his servants shall serve him.

Genesis 3:16-19. Unto the woman he said, I will greatly multiply thy sorrow and thy conception; in sorrow thou shalt bring forth children; and thy desire shall be to thy husband, and he shall rule over thee. And unto Adam he said, Because thou hast hearkened unto the voice of thy wife, and hast eaten of the tree, of which I commanded thee, saying, Thou shalt not eat of it: cursed is the ground for thy sake; in sorrow shalt thou eat of it all the days of thy life; Thorns also and thistles shall it bring forth to thee; and thou shalt eat the herb of the field; In the sweat of thy face shalt thou eat bread, till thou return unto the ground; for out of it wast thou taken: for dust thou art, and unto dust shalt thou return.

Job 5:7. Yet man is born unto trouble, as the sparks fly

upward.

Ecclesiastes 2:22-23. For what hath man of all his labour, and of the vexation of his heart, wherein he hath laboured under the sun? For all his days are sorrows, and his travail grief; yea, his heart taketh not rest in the night. This is also vanity.

Romans 8:18-23. For I reckon that the sufferings of this present time are not worthy to be compared with the glory which shall be revealed in us. For the earnest expectation of the creature waiteth for the manifestation of the sons of God. For the creature was made subject to vanity, not willingly, but by reason of him who hath subjected the same in hope, Because the creature itself also shall be delivered from the bondage of corruption into the glorious liberty of the children of God. For we know that the whole creation groaneth and travaileth in pain together until now. And not only they, but ourselves also, which have the firstfruits of the Spirit, even we ourselves groan within ourselves, waiting for the adoption, to wit, the redemption of our body.

[51] Ezekiel 18:4. Behold, all souls are mine; as the soul of the father, so also the soul of the son is mine: the soul that sinneth, it shall die.

Romans 5:12. Wherefore, as by one man sin entered into the world, and death by sin; and so death passed upon all men, for that all have sinned:

Romans 6:23. For the wages of sin is death; but the gift of God is eternal life through Jesus Christ our Lord.

[52] Matthew 25:41, 46. Then shall he say also unto them on the left hand, Depart from me, ye cursed, into everlasting fire, prepared for the devil and his angels.... And these shall go away into everlasting punishment: but the righteous into life eternal.

2 Thessalonians 1:9. Who shall be punished with everlasting destruction from the presence of the Lord, and from the glory of his power;

Revelation 14:9-11. And the third angel followed them,

saying with a loud voice, If any man worship the beast and his image, and receive his mark in his forehead, or in his hand, The same shall drink of the wine of the wrath of God, which is poured out without mixture into the cup of his indignation; and he shall be tormented with fire and brimstone in the presence of the holy angels, and in the presence of the Lamb: And the smoke of their torment ascendeth up for ever and ever: and they have no rest day nor night, who worship the beast and his image, and whosoever receiveth the mark of his name.

[53] **Q20**. Acts 13:48. And when the Gentiles heard this, they were glad, and glorified the word of the Lord: and as many as were ordained to eternal life believed.

Ephesians 1:4-5. According as he hath chosen us in him before the foundation of the world, that we should be holy and without blame before him in love: Having predestinated us unto the adoption of children by Jesus Christ to himself, according to the good pleasure of his will,

2 Thessalonians 2:13-14. But we are bound to give thanks alway to God for you, brethren beloved of the Lord, because God hath from the beginning chosen you to salvation through sanctification of the Spirit and belief of the truth: Whereunto he called you by our gospel, to the obtaining of the glory of our Lord Jesus Christ.

[54] Genesis 3:15. And I will put enmity between thee and the woman, and between thy seed and her seed; it shall bruise thy head, and thou shalt bruise his heel.

Genesis 17:7. And I will establish my covenant between me and thee and thy seed after thee in their generations for an everlasting covenant, to be a God unto thee, and to thy seed after thee.

Exodus 19:5-6. Now therefore, if ye will obey my voice indeed, and keep my covenant, then ye shall be a peculiar treasure unto me above all people: for all the earth is mine: And ye shall be unto me a kingdom of priests, and an holy nation. These are the words which thou shalt speak unto the children of Israel.

Jeremiah 31:31-34. Behold, the days come, saith the LORD, that I will make a new covenant with the house of Israel, and with the house of Judah: Not according to the covenant that I made with their fathers in the day that I took them by the hand to bring them out of the land of Egypt; which my covenant they brake, although I was an husband unto them, saith the LORD: But this shall be the covenant that I will make with the house of Israel; After those days, saith the LORD, I will put my law in their inward parts, and write it in their hearts; and will be their God, and they shall be my people. And they shall teach no more every man his neighbour, and every man his brother, saying, Know the LORD: for they shall all know me, from the least of them unto the greatest of them, saith the LORD: for I will forgive their iniquity, and I will remember their sin no more.

Matthew 20:28. Even as the Son of man came not to be ministered unto, but to minister, and to give his life a ransom for many.

1 Corinthians 11:25. After the same manner also he took the cup, when he had supped, saying, This cup is the new testament in my blood: this do ye, as oft as ye drink it, in remembrance of me.

Hebrews 9:15. And for this cause he is the mediator of the new testament, that by means of death, for the redemption of the transgressions that were under the first testament, they which are called might receive the promise of eternal inheritance.

Q21. John 14:6. Jesus saith unto him, I am the way, the truth, and the life: no man cometh unto the Father, but by me.

Acts 4:12. Neither is there salvation in any other: for there is none other name under heaven given among men, whereby we must be saved.

1 Timothy 2:5-6. For there is one God, and one mediator

between God and men, the man Christ Jesus; Who gave himself a ransom for all, to be testified in due time.

⁵⁶   Psalm 2:7. I will declare the decree: the LORD hath said unto me, Thou art my Son; this day have I begotten thee.

Matthew 3:17. And lo a voice from heaven, saying, This is my beloved Son, in whom I am well pleased.

Matthew 17:5. While he yet spake, behold, a bright cloud overshadowed them: and behold a voice out of the cloud, which said, This is my beloved Son, in whom I am well pleased; hear ye him.

John 1:18. No man hath seen God at any time; the only begotten Son, which is in the bosom of the Father, he hath declared him.

⁵⁷   Isaiah 9:6. For unto us a child is born, unto us a son is given: and the government shall be upon his shoulder: and his name shall be called Wonderful, Counsellor, The mighty God, The everlasting Father, The Prince of Peace.

Matthew 1:23. Behold, a virgin shall be with child, and shall bring forth a son, and they shall call his name Emmanuel, which being interpreted is, God with us.

John 1:14. And the Word was made flesh, and dwelt among us, (and we beheld his glory, the glory as of the only begotten of the Father,) full of grace and truth.

Galatians 4:4. But when the fulness of the time was come, God sent forth his Son, made of a woman, made under the law

⁵⁸   Acts 1:11. Which also said, Ye men of Galilee, why stand ye gazing up into heaven? this same Jesus, which is taken up from you into heaven, shall so come in like manner as ye have seen him go into heaven.

Hebrews 7:24-25. But this man, because he continueth ever, hath an unchangeable priesthood. Wherefore he is able also to save them to the uttermost that come unto God by him, seeing he ever liveth to make intercession for them.

⁵⁹ **Q22**. Philippians 2:7. But made himself of no reputation, and took upon him the form of a servant, and was made in the likeness of men:

Hebrews 2:14, 17. Forasmuch then as the children are partakers of flesh and blood, he also himself likewise took part of the same; that through death he might destroy him that had the power of death, that is, the devil.... Wherefore in all things it behoved him to be made like unto his brethren, that he might be a merciful and faithful high priest in things pertaining to God, to make reconciliation for the sins of the people.

⁶⁰ Luke 1:27, 31, 35. To a virgin espoused to a man whose name was Joseph, of the house of David; and the virgin's name was Mary.... And, behold, thou shalt conceive in thy womb, and bring forth a son, and shalt call his name JESUS.... And the angel answered and said unto her, The Holy Ghost shall come upon thee, and the power of the Highest shall overshadow thee: therefore also that holy thing which shall be born of thee shall be called the Son of God.

⁶¹ 2 Corinthians 5:21. For he hath made him to be sin for us, who knew no sin; that we might be made the righteousness of God in him.

Hebrews 4:15. For we have not an high priest which cannot be touched with the feeling of our infirmities; but was in all points tempted like as we are, yet without sin.

Hebrews 7:26. For such an high priest became us, who is holy, harmless, undefiled, separate from sinners, and made higher than the heavens;

1 John 3:5. And ye know that he was manifested to take away our sins; and in him is no sin.

⁶² **Q23**. Deuteronomy 18:18. I will raise them up a Prophet from among their brethren, like unto thee, and will put my words in his mouth; and he shall speak unto them all that I shall command him.

Acts 2:33. Therefore being by the right hand of God exalted, and having received of the Father the promise of the Holy Ghost, he hath shed forth this, which ye now see and hear.

Acts 3:22-23. For Moses truly said unto the fathers, A prophet shall the Lord your God raise up unto you of your brethren, like unto me; him shall ye hear in all things whatsoever he shall say unto you. And it shall come to pass, that every soul, which will not hear that prophet, shall be destroyed from among the people.

Hebrews 1:1-2. God, who at sundry times and in divers manners spake in time past unto the fathers by the prophets, Hath in these last days spoken unto us by his Son, whom he hath appointed heir of all things, by whom also he made the worlds

Hebrews 4:14-15. Seeing then that we have a great high priest, that is passed into the heavens, Jesus the Son of God, let us hold fast our profession. For we have not an high priest which cannot be touched with the feeling of our infirmities; but was in all points tempted like as we are, yet without sin.

Hebrews 5:5-6. So also Christ glorified not himself to be made an high priest; but he that said unto him, Thou art my Son, to day have I begotten thee. As he saith also in another place, Thou art a priest for ever after the order of Melchisedec.

Isaiah 9:6-7. For unto us a child is born, unto us a son is given: and the government shall be upon his shoulder: and his name shall be called Wonderful, Counsellor, The mighty God, The everlasting Father, The Prince of Peace. Of the increase of his government and peace there shall be no end, upon the throne of David, and upon his kingdom, to order it, and to establish it with judgment and with justice from henceforth even for ever. The zeal of the LORD of hosts will perform this.

Luke 1:32-33. He shall be great, and shall be called the Son of the Highest: and the Lord God shall give unto him the throne of his father David: And he shall reign over the house of

Jacob for ever; and of his kingdom there shall be no end.

John 18:37. Pilate therefore said unto him, Art thou a king then? Jesus answered, Thou sayest that I am a king. To this end was I born, and for this cause came I into the world, that I should bear witness unto the truth. Every one that is of the truth heareth my voice.

1 Corinthians 15:25. For he must reign, till he hath put all enemies under his feet.

[65] **Q24**. Luke 4:18-19, 21. The Spirit of the Lord is upon me, because he hath anointed me to preach the gospel to the poor; he hath sent me to heal the brokenhearted, to preach deliverance to the captives, and recovering of sight to the blind, to set at liberty them that are bruised, To preach the acceptable year of the Lord.... And he began to say unto them, This day is this scripture fulfilled in your ears.

Acts 1:1-2. The former treatise have I made, O Theophilus, of all that Jesus began both to do and teach, Until the day in which he was taken up, after that he through the Holy Ghost had given commandments unto the apostles whom he had chosen:

Hebrews 2:3. How shall we escape, if we neglect so great salvation; which at the first began to be spoken by the Lord, and was confirmed unto us by them that heard him

[66] John 15:26-27. But when the Comforter is come, whom I will send unto you from the Father, even the Spirit of truth, which proceedeth from the Father, he shall testify of me: And ye also shall bear witness, because ye have been with me from the beginning.

Acts 1:8. But ye shall receive power, after that the Holy Ghost is come upon you: and ye shall be witnesses unto me both in Jerusalem, and in all Judaea, and in Samaria, and unto the uttermost part of the earth.

1 Peter 1:11. Searching what, or what manner of time the

Spirit of Christ which was in them did signify, when it testified beforehand the sufferings of Christ, and the glory that should follow.

[67] John 4:41-42. And many more believed because of his own word; And said unto the woman, Now we believe, not because of thy saying: for we have heard him ourselves, and know that this is indeed the Christ, the Saviour of the world.

John 20:30-31. And many other signs truly did Jesus in the presence of his disciples, which are not written in this book: But these are written, that ye might believe that Jesus is the Christ, the Son of God; and that believing ye might have life through his name.

[68] **Q25**. Isaiah 53. Who hath believed our report? and to whom is the arm of the LORD revealed? For he shall grow up before him as a tender plant, and as a root out of a dry ground: he hath no form nor comeliness; and when we shall see him, there is no beauty that we should desire him. He is despised and rejected of men; a man of sorrows, and acquainted with grief: and we hid as it were our faces from him; he was despised, and we esteemed him not. Surely he hath borne our griefs, and carried our sorrows: yet we did esteem him stricken, smitten of God, and afflicted. But he was wounded for our transgressions, he was bruised for our iniquities: the chastisement of our peace was upon him; and with his stripes we are healed. All we like sheep have gone astray; we have turned every one to his own way; and the LORD hath laid on him the iniquity of us all. He was oppressed, and he was afflicted, yet he opened not his mouth: he is brought as a lamb to the slaughter, and as a sheep before her shearers is dumb, so he openeth not his mouth. He was taken from prison and from judgment: and who shall declare his generation? for he was cut off out of the land of the living: for the transgression of my people was he stricken. And he made his grave with the wicked, and with the rich in his death; because he had done no violence,

neither was any deceit in his mouth. Yet it pleased the LORD to bruise him; he hath put him to grief: when thou shalt make his soul an offering for sin, he shall see his seed, he shall prolong his days, and the pleasure of the LORD shall prosper in his hand. He shall see of the travail of his soul, and shall be satisfied: by his knowledge shall my righteous servant justify many; for he shall bear their iniquities. Therefore will I divide him a portion with the great, and he shall divide the spoil with the strong; because he hath poured out his soul unto death: and he was numbered with the transgressors; and he bare the sin of many, and made intercession for the transgressors.

Acts 8:32-35. The place of the scripture which he read was this, He was led as a sheep to the slaughter; and like a lamb dumb before his shearer, so opened he not his mouth: In his humiliation his judgment was taken away: and who shall declare his generation? for his life is taken from the earth. And the eunuch answered Philip, and said, I pray thee, of whom speaketh the prophet this? of himself, or of some other man? Then Philip opened his mouth, and began at the same scripture, and preached unto him Jesus.

Hebrews 9:26-28. For then must he often have suffered since the foundation of the world: but now once in the end of the world hath he appeared to put away sin by the sacrifice of himself. And as it is appointed unto men once to die, but after this the judgment: So Christ was once offered to bear the sins of many; and unto them that look for him shall he appear the second time without sin unto salvation.

Hebrews 10:12. But this man, after he had offered one sacrifice for sins for ever, sat down on the right hand of God

Romans 5:10-11. For if, when we were enemies, we were reconciled to God by the death of his Son, much more, being reconciled, we shall be saved by his life. And not only so, but we also joy in God through our Lord Jesus Christ, by whom we have now received the atonement.

2 Corinthians 5:18. And all things are of God, who hath reconciled us to himself by Jesus Christ, and hath given to us the ministry of reconciliation;

Colossians 1:21-22. And you, that were sometime alienated and enemies in your mind by wicked works, yet now hath he reconciled In the body of his flesh through death, to present you holy and unblameable and unreproveable in his sight.

Romans 8:34. Who is he that condemneth? It is Christ that died, yea rather, that is risen again, who is even at the right hand of God, who also maketh intercession for us.

Hebrews 7:25. Wherefore he is able also to save them to the uttermost that come unto God by him, seeing he ever liveth to make intercession for them.

Hebrews 9:24. For Christ is not entered into the holy places made with hands, which are the figures of the true; but into heaven itself, now to appear in the presence of God for us.

Q26. Psalm 110:3. Thy people shall be willing in the day of thy power, in the beauties of holiness from the womb of the morning: thou hast the dew of thy youth.

Matthew 28:18-20. And Jesus came and spake unto them, saying, All power is given unto me in heaven and in earth. Go ye therefore, and teach all nations, baptizing them in the name of the Father, and of the Son, and of the Holy Ghost: Teaching them to observe all things whatsoever I have commanded you: and, lo, I am with you alway, even unto the end of the world. Amen.

John 17:2. As thou hast given him power over all flesh, that he should give eternal life to as many as thou hast given him.

Colossians 1:13. Who hath delivered us from the power of darkness, and hath translated us into the kingdom of his dear Son.

Psalm 2:6-9. Yet have I set my king upon my holy hill of Zion. I will declare the decree: the LORD hath said unto me, Thou art my Son; this day have I begotten thee. Ask of me, and I shall give thee the heathen for thine inheritance, and the uttermost parts of the earth for thy possession. Thou shalt break them with a rod of iron; thou shalt dash them in pieces like a potter's vessel.

Psalm 110:1-2. The LORD said unto my Lord, Sit thou at my right hand, until I make thine enemies thy footstool. The LORD shall send the rod of thy strength out of Zion: rule thou in the midst of thine enemies.

Matthew 12:28. But if I cast out devils by the Spirit of God, then the kingdom of God is come unto you.

1 Corinthians 15:24-26. Then cometh the end, when he shall have delivered up the kingdom to God, even the Father; when he shall have put down all rule and all authority and power. For he must reign, till he hath put all enemies under his feet. The last enemy that shall be destroyed is death.

Colossians 2:15. And having spoiled principalities and powers, he made a show of them openly, triumphing over them in it.

[73] **Q27**. Luke 2:7. And she brought forth her firstborn son, and wrapped him in swaddling clothes, and laid him in a manger; because there was no room for them in the inn.

2 Corinthians 8:9. For ye know the grace of our Lord Jesus Christ, that, though he was rich, yet for your sakes he became poor, that ye through his poverty might be rich.

Galatians 4:4. But when the fulness of the time was come, God sent forth his Son, made of a woman, made under the law

[74] Galatians 4:4. But when the fulness of the time was come, God sent forth his Son, made of a woman, made under the law

[75] Isaiah 53:3. He is despised and rejected of men; a man of sorrows, and acquainted with grief: and we hid as it were our faces from him; he was despised, and we esteemed him not.

Luke 9:58. And Jesus said unto him, Foxes have holes, and birds of the air have nests; but the Son of man hath not where to lay his head.

John 4:6. Now Jacob's well was there. Jesus therefore, being wearied with his journey, sat thus on the well: and it was about the sixth hour.

John 11:35. Jesus wept.

Hebrews 2:18. For in that he himself hath suffered being tempted, he is able to succour them that are tempted.

Psalm 22:1. My God, my God, why hast thou forsaken me? why art thou so far from helping me, and from the words of my roaring?

Matthew 27:46. And about the ninth hour Jesus cried with a loud voice, saying, Eli, Eli, lama sabachthani? that is to say, My God, my God, why hast thou forsaken me?

Isaiah 53:10. Yet it pleased the LORD to bruise him; he hath put him to grief: when thou shalt make his soul an offering for sin, he shall see his seed, he shall prolong his days, and the pleasure of the LORD shall prosper in his hand.

1 John 2:2. And he is the propitiation for our sins: and not for ours only, but also for the sins of the whole world.

Galatians 3:13. Christ hath redeemed us from the curse of the law, being made a curse for us: for it is written, Cursed is every one that hangeth on a tree:

Philippians 2:8. And being found in fashion as a man, he humbled himself, and became obedient unto death, even the death of the cross.

Matthew 12:40. For as Jonas was three days and three nights in the whale's belly; so shall the Son of man be three days and three nights in the heart of the earth.

1 Corinthians 15:3-4. For I delivered unto you first of all that which I also received, how that Christ died for our sins according to the scriptures; And that he was buried, and that he rose again the third day according to the scriptures.

Q28. 1 Corinthians 15:4. And that he was buried, and that he rose again the third day according to the scriptures.

[80] Psalm 68:18. Thou hast ascended on high, thou hast led captivity captive: thou hast received gifts for men; yea, for the rebellious also, that the LORD God might dwell among them.

Acts 1:11. Which also said, Ye men of Galilee, why stand ye gazing up into heaven? this same Jesus, which is taken up from you into heaven, shall so come in like manner as ye have seen him go into heaven.

Ephesians 4:8. Wherefore he saith, When he ascended up on high, he led captivity captive, and gave gifts unto men.

[81] Psalm 110:1. The LORD said unto my Lord, Sit thou at my right hand, until I make thine enemies thy footstool.

Acts 2:33-34. Therefore being by the right hand of God exalted, and having received of the Father the promise of the Holy Ghost, he hath shed forth this, which ye now see and hear. For David is not ascended into the heavens: but he saith himself, The Lord said unto my Lord, Sit thou on my right hand,

Hebrews 1:3. Who being the brightness of his glory, and the express image of his person, and upholding all things by the word of his power, when he had by himself purged our sins, sat down on the right hand of the Majesty on high

[82] Matthew 16:27. For the Son of man shall come in the glory of his Father with his angels; and then he shall reward every man according to his works.

Acts 17:31. Because he hath appointed a day, in the which he will judge the world in righteousness by that man whom he hath ordained; whereof he hath given assurance unto all men, in that he hath raised him from the dead.

[83] **Q29**. Titus 3:4-7. But after that the kindness and love of God our Saviour toward man appeared, Not by works of righteousness which we have done, but according to his mercy he saved us, by the washing of regeneration, and renewing of the Holy Ghost; Which he shed on us abundantly through Jesus Christ our Saviour; That being justified by his grace, we should

be made heirs according to the hope of eternal life.

Q30. Romans 10:17. So then faith cometh by hearing, and hearing by the word of God.

1 Corinthians 2:12-16. Now we have received, not the spirit of the world, but the spirit which is of God; that we might know the things that are freely given to us of God. Which things also we speak, not in the words which man's wisdom teacheth, but which the Holy Ghost teacheth; comparing spiritual things with spiritual. But the natural man receiveth not the things of the Spirit of God: for they are foolishness unto him: neither can he know them, because they are spiritually discerned. But he that is spiritual judgeth all things, yet he himself is judged of no man. For who hath known the mind of the Lord, that he may instruct him? But we have the mind of Christ.

Ephesians 2:8. For by grace are ye saved through faith; and that not of yourselves: it is the gift of God:

Philippians 1:29. For unto you it is given in the behalf of Christ, not only to believe on him, but also to suffer for his sake

John 15:5. I am the vine, ye are the branches: He that abideth in me, and I in him, the same bringeth forth much fruit: for without me ye can do nothing.

1 Corinthians 1:9. God is faithful, by whom ye were called unto the fellowship of his Son Jesus Christ our Lord.

Ephesians 3:17. That Christ may dwell in your hearts by faith; that ye, being rooted and grounded in love

Q31. Acts 26:18. To open their eyes, and to turn them from darkness to light, and from the power of Satan unto God, that they may receive forgiveness of sins, and inheritance among them which are sanctified by faith that is in me.

1 Corinthians 2:10, 12. But God hath revealed them unto us by his Spirit: for the Spirit searcheth all things, yea, the deep things of God.... Now we have received, not the spirit of the world, but the spirit which is of God; that we might know the

things that are freely given to us of God.

2 Corinthians 4:6. For God, who commanded the light to shine out of darkness, hath shined in our hearts, to give the light of the knowledge of the glory of God in the face of Jesus Christ.

Ephesians 1:17-18. That the God of our Lord Jesus Christ, the Father of glory, may give unto you the spirit of wisdom and revelation in the knowledge of him: The eyes of your understanding being enlightened; that ye may know what is the hope of his calling, and what the riches of the glory of his inheritance in the saints

Deuteronomy 30:6. And the LORD thy God will circumcise thine heart, and the heart of thy seed, to love the LORD thy God with all thine heart, and with all thy soul, that thou mayest live.

Ezekiel 36:26-27. A new heart also will I give you, and a new spirit will I put within you: and I will take away the stony heart out of your flesh, and I will give you an heart of flesh. And I will put my spirit within you, and cause you to walk in my statutes, and ye shall keep my judgments, and do them.

John 3:5. Jesus answered, Verily, verily, I say unto thee, Except a man be born of water and of the Spirit, he cannot enter into the kingdom of God.

Titus 3:5. Not by works of righteousness which we have done, but according to his mercy he saved us, by the washing of regeneration, and renewing of the Holy Ghost

John 6:44-45. No man can come to me, except the Father which hath sent me draw him: and I will raise him up at the last day. It is written in the prophets, And they shall be all taught of God. Every man therefore that hath heard, and hath learned of the Father, cometh unto me.

Acts 16:14. And a certain woman named Lydia, a seller of purple, of the city of Thyatira, which worshipped God, heard us: whose heart the Lord opened, that she attended unto the things which were spoken of Paul.

[89] Isaiah 45:22. Look unto me, and be ye saved, all the ends of the earth: for I am God, and there is none else.

Matthew 11:28-30. Come unto me, all ye that labour and are heavy laden, and I will give you rest. Take my yoke upon you, and learn of me; for I am meek and lowly in heart: and ye shall find rest unto your souls. For my yoke is easy, and my burden is light.

Revelation 22:17. And the Spirit and the bride say, Come. And let him that heareth say, Come. And let him that is athirst come. And whosoever will, let him take the water of life freely.

[90] **Q32**. Romans 8:30. Moreover whom he did predestinate, them he also called: and whom he called, them he also justified: and whom he justified, them he also glorified.

1 Corinthians 1:30. But of him are ye in Christ Jesus, who of God is made unto us wisdom, and righteousness, and sanctification, and redemption:

1 Corinthians 6:11. And such were some of you: but ye are washed, but ye are sanctified, but ye are justified in the name of the Lord Jesus, and by the Spirit of our God.

Ephesians 1:5. Having predestinated us unto the adoption of children by Jesus Christ to himself, according to the good pleasure of his will

[91] **Q33**. Romans 3:24. Being justified freely by his grace through the redemption that is in Christ Jesus.

[92] Romans 4:6-8. Even as David also describeth the blessedness of the man, unto whom God imputeth righteousness without works, Saying, Blessed are they whose iniquities are forgiven, and whose sins are covered. Blessed is the man to whom the Lord will not impute sin.

2 Corinthians 5:19. To wit, that God was in Christ, reconciling the world unto himself, not imputing their trespasses unto them; and hath committed unto us the word of reconciliation.

[93] 2 Corinthians 5:21. For he hath made him to be sin for us, who knew no sin; that we might be made the righteousness of God in him.

[94] Romans 4:6, 11. Even as David also describeth the blessedness of the man, unto whom God imputeth righteousness without works.... And he received the sign of circumcision, a seal of the righteousness of the faith which he had yet being uncircumcised: that he might be the father of all them that believe, though they be not circumcised; that righteousness might be imputed unto them also:

Romans 5:19. For as by one man's disobedience many were made sinners, so by the obedience of one shall many be made righteous.

[95] Galatians 2:16. Knowing that a man is not justified by the works of the law, but by the faith of Jesus Christ, even we have believed in Jesus Christ, that we might be justified by the faith of Christ, and not by the works of the law: for by the works of the law shall no flesh be justified.

Philippians 3:9. And be found in him, not having mine own righteousness, which is of the law, but that which is through the faith of Christ, the righteousness which is of God by faith.

[96] **Q34**. 1 John 3:1. Behold, what manner of love the Father hath bestowed upon us, that we should be called the sons of God: therefore the world knoweth us not, because it knew him not.

John 1:12 But as many as received him, to them gave he power to become the sons of God, even to them that believe on his name.

Rom. 8:17 And if children, then heirs; heirs of God, and joint-heirs with Christ; if so be that we suffer with him, that we may be also glorified together.

[97] **Q35**. Ezekiel 36:27. And I will put my spirit within you, and cause you to walk in my statutes, and ye shall keep my judgments, and do them.

Philippians 2:13. For it is God which worketh in you both to will and to do of his good pleasure.

2 Thessalonians 2:13. But we are bound to give thanks alway to God for you, brethren beloved of the Lord, because God hath from the beginning chosen you to salvation through sanctification of the Spirit and belief of the truth.

[98] 2 Corinthians 5:17. Therefore if any man be in Christ, he is a new creature: old things are passed away; behold, all things are become new.

Ephesians 4:23-24. And be renewed in the spirit of your mind; And that ye put on the new man, which after God is created in righteousness and true holiness.

1 Thessalonians 5:23. And the very God of peace sanctify you wholly; and I pray God your whole spirit and soul and body be preserved blameless unto the coming of our Lord Jesus Christ.

[99] Ezekiel 36:25-27. Then will I sprinkle clean water upon you, and ye shall be clean: from all your filthiness, and from all your idols, will I cleanse you. A new heart also will I give you, and a new spirit will I put within you: and I will take away the stony heart out of your flesh, and I will give you an heart of flesh. And I will put my spirit within you, and cause you to walk in my statutes, and ye shall keep my judgments, and do them.

Romans 6:4, 6, 12-14. Therefore we are buried with him by baptism into death: that like as Christ was raised up from the dead by the glory of the Father, even so we also should walk in newness of life.... Knowing this, that our old man is crucified with him, that the body of sin might be destroyed, that henceforth we should not serve sin.... Let not sin therefore reign in your mortal body, that ye should obey it in the lusts thereof. Neither yield ye your members as instruments of unrighteousness unto sin: but yield yourselves unto God, as those that are alive from the dead, and your members as instruments of righteousness unto God. For sin shall not have dominion over you: for ye are not under the law, but under grace.

2 Corinthians 7:1. Having therefore these promises, dearly beloved, let us cleanse ourselves from all filthiness of the flesh and spirit, perfecting holiness in the fear of God.

1 Peter 2:24. Who his own self bare our sins in his own body on the tree, that we, being dead to sins, should live unto righteousness: by whose stripes ye were healed.

Q36. Romans 5:5. And hope maketh not ashamed; because the love of God is shed abroad in our hearts by the Holy Ghost which is given unto us.

Romans 5:1. Therefore being justified by faith, we have peace with God through our Lord Jesus Christ.

Romans 14:17. For the kingdom of God is not meat and drink; but righteousness, and peace, and joy in the Holy Ghost.

2 Peter 3:18. But grow in grace, and in the knowledge of our Lord and Saviour Jesus Christ. To him be glory both now and for ever. Amen.

Philippians 1:6. Being confident of this very thing, that he which hath begun a good work in you will perform it until the day of Jesus Christ:

1 Peter 1:5. Who are kept by the power of God through faith unto salvation ready to be revealed in the last time.

Q37. Hebrews 12:23. To the general assembly and church of the firstborn, which are written in heaven, and to God the Judge of all, and to the spirits of just men made perfect

Luke 23:43. And Jesus said unto him, Verily I say unto thee, To day shalt thou be with me in paradise.

2 Corinthians 5:6, 8. Therefore we are always confident, knowing that, whilst we are at home in the body, we are absent from the Lord.... We are confident, I say, and willing rather to be absent from the body, and to be present with the Lord.

Philippians 1:23. For I am in a strait betwixt two, having a desire to depart, and to be with Christ; which is far better.

[107] 1 Thessalonians 4:14. For if we believe that Jesus died and rose again, even so them also which sleep in Jesus will God bring with him.

[108] Daniel 12:2. And many of them that sleep in the dust of the earth shall awake, some to everlasting life, and some to shame and everlasting contempt.

John 5:28-29. Marvel not at this: for the hour is coming, in the which all that are in the graves shall hear his voice, And shall come forth; they that have done good, unto the resurrection of life; and they that have done evil, unto the resurrection of damnation.

Acts 24:15. And have hope toward God, which they themselves also allow, that there shall be a resurrection of the dead, both of the just and unjust.

[109] **Q38**. 1 Corinthians 15:42-43. So also is the resurrection of the dead. It is sown in corruption; it is raised in incorruption: It is sown in dishonour; it is raised in glory: it is sown in weakness; it is raised in power.

[110] Matthew 25:33-34, 46. And he shall set the sheep on his right hand, but the goats on the left. Then shall the King say unto them on his right hand, Come, ye blessed of my Father, inherit the kingdom prepared for you from the foundation of the world.... And these shall go away into everlasting punishment: but the righteous into life eternal.

[111] Romans 8:29. For whom he did foreknow, he also did predestinate to be conformed to the image of his Son, that he might be the firstborn among many brethren.

1 John 3:2. Beloved, now are we the sons of God, and it doth not yet appear what we shall be: but we know that, when he shall appear, we shall be like him; for we shall see him as he is.

[112] Psalm 16:11. Thou wilt show me the path of life: in thy presence is fulness of joy; at thy right hand there are pleasures for evermore.

1 Thessalonians 4:17. Then we which are alive and remain shall be caught up together with them in the clouds, to meet the Lord in the air: and so shall we ever be with the Lord.

Q39. Deuteronomy 29:29. The secret things belong unto the LORD our God: but those things which are revealed belong unto us and to our children for ever, that we may do all the words of this law.

Micah 6:8. He hath showed thee, O man, what is good; and what doth the LORD require of thee, but to do justly, and to love mercy, and to walk humbly with thy God?

1 John 5:2-3. By this we know that we love the children of God, when we love God, and keep his commandments. For this is the love of God, that we keep his commandments: and his commandments are not grievous.

Q40. Romans 2:14-15. For when the Gentiles, which have not the law, do by nature the things contained in the law, these, having not the law, are a law unto themselves: Which show the work of the law written in their hearts, their conscience also bearing witness, and their thoughts the mean while accusing or else excusing one another;)

Romans 10:5. For Moses describeth the righteousness which is of the law, That the man which doeth those things shall live by them.

Q41. Deuteronomy 4:13. And he declared unto you his covenant, which he commanded you to perform, even ten commandments; and he wrote them upon two tables of stone.

Matthew 19:17-19. And he said unto him, Why callest thou me good? there is none good but one, that is, God: but if thou wilt enter into life, keep the commandments. He saith unto him, Which? Jesus said, Thou shalt do no murder, Thou shalt not commit adultery, Thou shalt not steal, Thou shalt not bear false witness, Honour thy father and thy mother: and, Thou shalt love thy neighbour as thyself.

Q42. Matthew 22:37-40. Jesus said unto him, Thou shalt love the Lord thy God with all thy heart, and with all thy soul, and with all thy mind. This is the first and great commandment. And the second is like unto it, Thou shalt love thy neighbour as thyself. On these two commandments hang all the law and the prophets.

Q43. Exodus 20:2. I am the LORD thy God, which have brought thee out of the land of Egypt, out of the house of bondage.

Deuteronomy 5:6. I am the LORD thy God, which brought thee out of the land of Egypt, from the house of bondage.

Q44. Luke 1:74-75. That he would grant unto us, that we being delivered out of the hand of our enemies might serve him without fear, In holiness and righteousness before him, all the days of our life.

1 Peter 1:14-19. As obedient children, not fashioning yourselves according to the former lusts in your ignorance: But as he which hath called you is holy, so be ye holy in all manner of conversation; Because it is written, Be ye holy; for I am holy. And if ye call on the Father, who without respect of persons judgeth according to every man's work, pass the time of your sojourning here in fear: Forasmuch as ye know that ye were not redeemed with corruptible things, as silver and gold, from your vain conversation received by tradition from your fathers; But with the precious blood of Christ, as of a lamb without blemish and without spot.

Q45. Exodus 20:3. Thou shalt have no other gods before me.

Deuteronomy 5:7. Thou shalt have none other gods before me.

Q46. 1 Chronicles 28:9. And thou, Solomon my son, know thou the God of thy father, and serve him with a perfect heart and with a willing mind: for the LORD searcheth all hearts, and understandeth all the imaginations of the thoughts: if thou seek him, he will be found of thee; but if thou forsake him, he will cast thee off for ever.

Isaiah 45:20-25. Assemble yourselves and come; draw near together, ye that are escaped of the nations: they have no knowledge that set up the wood of their graven image, and pray unto a god that cannot save. Tell ye, and bring them near; yea, let them take counsel together: who hath declared this from ancient time? who hath told it from that time? have not I the LORD? and there is no God else beside me; a just God and a Saviour; there is none beside me. Look unto me, and be ye saved, all the ends of the earth: for I am God, and there is none else. I have sworn by myself, the word is gone out of my mouth in righteousness, and shall not return, That unto me every knee shall bow, every tongue shall swear. Surely, shall one say, in the LORD have I righteousness and strength: even to him shall men come; and all that are incensed against him shall be ashamed. In the LORD shall all the seed of Israel be justified, and shall glory.

Matthew 4:10. Then saith Jesus unto him, Get thee hence, Satan: for it is written, Thou shalt worship the Lord thy God, and him only shalt thou serve.

[121] **Q47**. Psalm 14:1. The fool hath said in his heart, There is no God. They are corrupt, they have done abominable works, there is none that doeth good.

[122] Romans 1:20-21. For the invisible things of him from the creation of the world are clearly seen, being understood by the things that are made, even his eternal power and Godhead; so that they are without excuse: Because that, when they knew God, they glorified him not as God, neither were thankful; but became vain in their imaginations, and their foolish heart was darkened.

[123] Psalm 81:10-11. I am the LORD thy God, which brought thee out of the land of Egypt: open thy mouth wide, and I will fill it. But my people would not hearken to my voice; and Israel

would none of me.

[124] Ezekiel 8:16-18. And he brought me into the inner court of the LORD'S house, and, behold, at the door of the temple of the LORD, between the porch and the altar, were about five and twenty men, with their backs toward the temple of the LORD, and their faces toward the east; and they worshipped the sun toward the east. Then he said unto me, Hast thou seen this, O son of man? Is it a light thing to the house of Judah that they commit the abominations which they commit here? for they have filled the land with violence, and have returned to provoke me to anger: and, lo, they put the branch to their nose. Therefore will I also deal in fury: mine eye shall not spare, neither will I have pity: and though they cry in mine ears with a loud voice, yet will I not hear them.

Romans 1:25. Who changed the truth of God into a lie, and worshipped and served the creature more than the Creator, who is blessed for ever. Amen.

[125] **Q48**. Deuteronomy 30:17-18. But if thine heart turn away, so that thou wilt not hear, but shalt be drawn away, and worship other gods, and serve them; I denounce unto you this day, that ye shall surely perish, and that ye shall not prolong your days upon the land, whither thou passest over Jordan to go to possess it.

Psalm 44:20-21. If we have forgotten the name of our God, or stretched out our hands to a strange god; Shall not God search this out? for he knoweth the secrets of the heart.

Ezekiel 8:12. Then said he unto me, Son of man, hast thou seen what the ancients of the house of Israel do in the dark, every man in the chambers of his imagery? for they say, The LORD seeth us not; the LORD hath forsaken the earth.

[126] **Q49**. Exodus 20:4-6. Thou shalt not make unto thee any graven image, or any likeness of any thing that is in heaven above, or that is in the earth beneath, or that is in the water under

the earth: Thou shalt not bow down thyself to them, nor serve them: for I the LORD thy God am a jealous God, visiting the iniquity of the fathers upon the children unto the third and fourth generation of them that hate me; And showing mercy unto thousands of them that love me, and keep my commandments.

Deuteronomy 5:8-10. Thou shalt not make thee any graven image, or any likeness of any thing that is in heaven above, or that is in the earth beneath, or that is in the waters beneath the earth: Thou shalt not bow down thyself unto them, nor serve them: for I the LORD thy God am a jealous God, visiting the iniquity of the fathers upon the children unto the third and fourth generation of them that hate me, And showing mercy unto thousands of them that love me and keep my commandments.

Q50. Deuteronomy 12:32. What thing soever I command you, observe to do it: thou shalt not add thereto, nor diminish from it.

Matthew 28:20. Teaching them to observe all things whatsoever I have commanded you: and, lo, I am with you alway, even unto the end of the world. Amen.

Q51. Deuteronomy 4:15-19. Take ye therefore good heed unto yourselves; for ye saw no manner of similitude on the day that the LORD spake unto you in Horeb out of the midst of the fire: Lest ye corrupt yourselves, and make you a graven image, the similitude of any figure, the likeness of male or female, The likeness of any beast that is on the earth, the likeness of any winged fowl that flieth in the air, The likeness of any thing that creepeth on the ground, the likeness of any fish that is in the waters beneath the earth: And lest thou lift up thine eyes unto heaven, and when thou seest the sun, and the moon, and the stars, even all the host of heaven, shouldest be driven to worship them, and serve them, which the LORD thy God hath divided unto all nations under the whole heaven.

Romans 1:22-23. Professing themselves to be wise, they became fools, And changed the glory of the uncorruptible God into an image made like to corruptible man, and to birds, and fourfooted beasts, and creeping things.

[129] Leviticus 10:1-2. And Nadab and Abihu, the sons of Aaron, took either of them his censer, and put fire therein, and put incense thereon, and offered strange fire before the LORD, which he commanded them not. And there went out fire from the LORD, and devoured them, and they died before the LORD.

Jeremiah 19:4-5. Because they have forsaken me, and have estranged this place, and have burned incense in it unto other gods, whom neither they nor their fathers have known, nor the kings of Judah, and have filled this place with the blood of innocents; They have built also the high places of Baal, to burn their sons with fire for burnt offerings unto Baal, which I commanded not, nor spake it, neither came it into my mind:

Colossians 2:18-23. Let no man beguile you of your reward in a voluntary humility and worshipping of angels, intruding into those things which he hath not seen, vainly puffed up by his fleshly mind, And not holding the Head, from which all the body by joints and bands having nourishment ministered, and knit together, increaseth with the increase of God. Wherefore if ye be dead with Christ from the rudiments of the world, why, as though living in the world, are ye subject to ordinances, Touch not; taste not; handle not; Which all are to perish with the using;) after the commandments and doctrines of men? Which things have indeed a show of wisdom in will worship, and humility, and neglecting of the body; not in any honour to the satisfying of the flesh.

[130] **Q52**. Psalm 95:2-3, 6-7. Let us come before his presence with thanksgiving, and make a joyful noise unto him with psalms. For the LORD is a great God, and a great King above all gods.... O come, let us worship and bow down: let us kneel before the

LORD our maker. For he is our God; and we are the people of his pasture, and the sheep of his hand. To day if ye will hear his voice,

Psalm 96:9-10. O worship the LORD in the beauty of holiness: fear before him, all the earth. Say among the heathen that the LORD reigneth: the world also shall be established that it shall not be moved: he shall judge the people righteously.

[131] Exodus 19:5. Now therefore, if ye will obey my voice indeed, and keep my covenant, then ye shall be a peculiar treasure unto me above all people: for all the earth is mine:

Psalm 45:11. So shall the king greatly desire thy beauty: for he is thy Lord; and worship thou him.

Isaiah 54:5. For thy Maker is thine husband; the LORD of hosts is his name; and thy Redeemer the Holy One of Israel; The God of the whole earth shall he be called.

[132] Exodus 34:14. For thou shalt worship no other god: for the LORD, whose name is Jealous, is a jealous God:

1 Corinthians 10:22. Do we provoke the Lord to jealousy? are we stronger than he?

[133] **Q53**. Exodus 20:7. Thou shalt not take the name of the LORD thy God in vain; for the LORD will not hold him guiltless that taketh his name in vain.

Deuteronomy 5:11. Thou shalt not take the name of the LORD thy God in vain: for the LORD will not hold him guiltless that taketh his name in vain.

[134] **Q54**. Deuteronomy 10:20. Thou shalt fear the LORD thy God; him shalt thou serve, and to him shalt thou cleave, and swear by his name.

Psalm 29:2. Give unto the LORD the glory due unto his name; worship the LORD in the beauty of holiness.

Matthew 6:9. After this manner therefore pray ye: Our Father which art in heaven, Hallowed be thy name.

[135] 1 Chronicles 29:10-13. Wherefore David blessed the

LORD before all the congregation: and David said, Blessed be thou, LORD God of Israel our father, for ever and ever. Thine, O LORD, is the greatness, and the power, and the glory, and the victory, and the majesty: for all that is in the heaven and in the earth is thine; thine is the kingdom, O LORD, and thou art exalted as head above all. Both riches and honour come of thee, and thou reignest over all; and in thine hand is power and might; and in thine hand it is to make great, and to give strength unto all. Now therefore, our God, we thank thee, and praise thy glorious name.

Revelation 15:3-4. And they sing the song of Moses the servant of God, and the song of the Lamb, saying, Great and marvellous are thy works, Lord God Almighty; just and true are thy ways, thou King of saints. Who shall not fear thee, O Lord, and glorify thy name? for thou only art holy: for all nations shall come and worship before thee; for thy judgments are made manifest.

[136] Acts 2:42. And they continued stedfastly in the apostles' doctrine and fellowship, and in breaking of bread, and in prayers.

1 Corinthians 11:27-28. Wherefore whosoever shall eat this bread, and drink this cup of the Lord, unworthily, shall be guilty of the body and blood of the Lord. But let a man examine himself, and so let him eat of that bread, and drink of that cup.

[137] Psalm 138:2. I will worship toward thy holy temple, and praise thy name for thy lovingkindness and for thy truth: for thou hast magnified thy word above all thy name.

Revelation 22:18-19. For I testify unto every man that heareth the words of the prophecy of this book, If any man shall add unto these things, God shall add unto him the plagues that are written in this book: And if any man shall take away from the words of the book of this prophecy, God shall take away his part out of the book of life, and out of the holy city, and from the things which are written in this book.

[138] Psalm 107:21-22. Oh that men would praise the LORD for

his goodness, and for his wonderful works to the children of men! And let them sacrifice the sacrifices of thanksgiving, and declare his works with rejoicing.

Revelation 4:11. Thou art worthy, O Lord, to receive glory and honour and power: for thou hast created all things, and for thy pleasure they are and were created.

[139] **Q55**. Leviticus 19:12. And ye shall not swear by my name falsely, neither shalt thou profane the name of thy God: I am the LORD.

Matthew 5:33-37. Again, ye have heard that it hath been said by them of old time, Thou shalt not forswear thyself, but shalt perform unto the Lord thine oaths: But I say unto you, Swear not at all; neither by heaven; for it is God's throne: Nor by the earth; for it is his footstool: neither by Jerusalem; for it is the city of the great King. Neither shalt thou swear by thy head, because thou canst not make one hair white or black. But let your communication be, Yea, yea; Nay, nay: for whatsoever is more than these cometh of evil.

James 5:12. But above all things, my brethren, swear not, neither by heaven, neither by the earth, neither by any other oath: but let your yea be yea; and your nay, nay; lest ye fall into condemnation.

[140] **Q56**. Deuteronomy 28:58-59. If thou wilt not observe to do all the words of this law that are written in this book, that thou mayest fear this glorious and fearful name, THE LORD THY GOD; Then the LORD will make thy plagues wonderful, and the plagues of thy seed, even great plagues, and of long continuance, and sore sicknesses, and of long continuance.

1 Samuel 3:13. For I have told him that I will judge his house for ever for the iniquity which he knoweth; because his sons made themselves vile, and he restrained them not.

1 Samuel 4:11. And the ark of God was taken; and the two sons of Eli, Hophni and Phinehas, were slain.

[141] **Q57**. Exodus 20:8-11. Remember the sabbath day, to keep it holy. Six days shalt thou labour, and do all thy work: But the seventh day is the sabbath of the LORD thy God: in it thou shalt not do any work, thou, nor thy son, nor thy daughter, thy manservant, nor thy maidservant, nor thy cattle, nor thy stranger that is within thy gates: For in six days the LORD made heaven and earth, the sea, and all that in them is, and rested the seventh day: wherefore the LORD blessed the sabbath day, and hallowed it.

Deuteronomy 5:12-15. Keep the sabbath day to sanctify it, as the LORD thy God hath commanded thee. Six days thou shalt labour, and do all thy work: But the seventh day is the sabbath of the LORD thy God: in it thou shalt not do any work, thou, nor thy son, nor thy daughter, nor thy manservant, nor thy maidservant, nor thine ox, nor thine ass, nor any of thy cattle, nor thy stranger that is within thy gates; that thy manservant and thy maidservant may rest as well as thou. And remember that thou wast a servant in the land of Egypt, and that the LORD thy God brought thee out thence through a mighty hand and by a stretched out arm: therefore the LORD thy God commanded thee to keep the sabbath day.

[142] **Q58**. Exodus 31:13, 16-17. Speak thou also unto the children of Israel, saying, Verily my sabbaths ye shall keep: for it is a sign between me and you throughout your generations; that ye may know that I am the LORD that doth sanctify you.... Wherefore the children of Israel shall keep the sabbath, to observe the sabbath throughout their generations, for a perpetual covenant. It is a sign between me and the children of Israel for ever: for in six days the LORD made heaven and earth, and on the seventh day he rested, and was refreshed.

[143] **Q59**. Genesis 2:2-3. And on the seventh day God ended his work which he had made; and he rested on the seventh day from all his work which he had made. And God blessed the

seventh day, and sanctified it: because that in it he had rested from all his work which God created and made.

Exodus 20:11. For in six days the LORD made heaven and earth, the sea, and all that in them is, and rested the seventh day: wherefore the LORD blessed the sabbath day, and hallowed it.

[144] Mark 2:27-28. And he said unto them, The sabbath was made for man, and not man for the sabbath: Therefore the Son of man is Lord also of the sabbath.

Acts 20:7. And upon the first day of the week, when the disciples came together to break bread, Paul preached unto them, ready to depart on the morrow; and continued his speech until midnight.

1 Corinthians 16:2. Upon the first day of the week let every one of you lay by him in store, as God hath prospered him, that there be no gatherings when I come.

Revelation 1:10. I was in the Spirit on the Lord's day, and heard behind me a great voice, as of a trumpet

[145] **Q60**. Exodus 20:10. But the seventh day is the sabbath of the LORD thy God: in it thou shalt not do any work, thou, nor thy son, nor thy daughter, thy manservant, nor thy maidservant, nor thy cattle, nor thy stranger that is within thy gates:

Nehemiah 13:15-22. In those days saw I in Judah some treading wine presses on the sabbath, and bringing in sheaves, and lading asses; as also wine, grapes, and figs, and all manner of burdens, which they brought into Jerusalem on the sabbath day: and I testified against them in the day wherein they sold victuals. There dwelt men of Tyre also therein, which brought fish, and all manner of ware, and sold on the sabbath unto the children of Judah, and in Jerusalem. Then I contended with the nobles of Judah, and said unto them, What evil thing is this that ye do, and profane the sabbath day? Did not your fathers thus, and did not our God bring all this evil upon us, and upon this city? yet ye bring more wrath upon Israel by profaning the sabbath. And it came to pass, that when the gates of Jerusalem began to be dark before the sabbath, I commanded that the gates should be shut, and charged that they should not be opened till after the sabbath: and some of my servants set I at the gates, that there should no burden be brought in on the sabbath day. So the merchants and sellers of all kind of ware lodged without Jerusalem once or twice. Then I testified against them, and said unto them, Why lodge ye about the wall? if ye do so again, I will lay hands on you. From that time forth came they no more on the sabbath. And I commanded the Levites that they should cleanse themselves, and that they should come and keep the gates, to sanctify the sabbath day. Remember me, O my God, concerning this also, and spare me according to the greatness of thy mercy.

Isaiah 58:13-14. If thou turn away thy foot from the sabbath, from doing thy pleasure on my holy day; and call the sabbath a delight, the holy of the LORD, honourable; and shalt honour him, not doing thine own ways, nor finding thine own pleasure, nor speaking thine own words: Then shalt thou delight thyself in the LORD; and I will cause thee to ride upon the high places of the earth, and feed thee with the heritage of Jacob thy father: for the mouth of the LORD hath spoken it.

146   Exodus 20:8. Remember the sabbath day, to keep it holy.

Leviticus 23:3. Six days shall work be done: but the seventh day is the sabbath of rest, an holy convocation; ye shall do no work therein: it is the sabbath of the LORD in all your dwellings.

Luke 4:16. And he came to Nazareth, where he had been brought up: and, as his custom was, he went into the synagogue on the sabbath day, and stood up for to read.

Acts 20:7. And upon the first day of the week, when the disciples came together to break bread, Paul preached unto them, ready to depart on the morrow; and continued his speech until midnight.

[147] Matthew 12:1-13. At that time Jesus went on the sabbath day through the corn; and his disciples were an hungred, and began to pluck the ears of corn, and to eat. But when the Pharisees saw it, they said unto him, Behold, thy disciples do that which is not lawful to do upon the sabbath day. But he said unto them, Have ye not read what David did, when he was an hungred, and they that were with him; How he entered into the house of God, and did eat the showbread, which was not lawful for him to eat, neither for them which were with him, but only for the priests? Or have ye not read in the law, how that on the sabbath days the priests in the temple profane the sabbath, and are blameless? But I say unto you, That in this place is one greater than the temple. But if ye had known what this meaneth, I will have mercy, and not sacrifice, ye would not have condemned the guiltless. For the Son of man is Lord even of the sabbath day. And when he was departed thence, he went into their synagogue: And, behold, there was a man which had his hand withered. And they asked him, saying, Is it lawful to heal on the sabbath days? that they might accuse him. And he said unto them, What man shall there be among you, that shall have one sheep, and if it fall into a pit on the sabbath day, will he not lay hold on it, and lift it out? How much then is a man better than a sheep? Wherefore it is lawful to do well on the sabbath days. Then saith he to the man, Stretch forth thine hand. And he stretched it forth; and it was restored whole, like as the other.

[148] **Q61**. Nehemiah 13:15-22. In those days saw I in Judah some treading wine presses on the sabbath, and bringing in sheaves, and lading asses; as also wine, grapes, and figs, and all manner of burdens, which they brought into Jerusalem on the sabbath day: and I testified against them in the day wherein they sold victuals. There dwelt men of Tyre also therein, which brought fish, and all manner of ware, and sold on the sabbath unto

the children of Judah, and in Jerusalem. Then I contended with the nobles of Judah, and said unto them, What evil thing is this that ye do, and profane the sabbath day? Did not your fathers thus, and did not our God bring all this evil upon us, and upon this city? yet ye bring more wrath upon Israel by profaning the sabbath. And it came to pass, that when the gates of Jerusalem began to be dark before the sabbath, I commanded that the gates should be shut, and charged that they should not be opened till after the sabbath: and some of my servants set I at the gates, that there should no burden be brought in on the sabbath day. So the merchants and sellers of all kind of ware lodged without Jerusalem once or twice. Then I testified against them, and said unto them, Why lodge ye about the wall? if ye do so again, I will lay hands on you. From that time forth came they no more on the sabbath. And I commanded the Levites that they should cleanse themselves, and that they should come and keep the gates, to sanctify the sabbath day. Remember me, O my God, concerning this also, and spare me according to the greatness of thy mercy.

Isaiah 58:13-14. If thou turn away thy foot from the sabbath, from doing thy pleasure on my holy day; and call the sabbath a delight, the holy of the LORD, honourable; and shalt honour him, not doing thine own ways, nor finding thine own pleasure, nor speaking thine own words: Then shalt thou delight thyself in the LORD; and I will cause thee to ride upon the high places of the earth, and feed thee with the heritage of Jacob thy father: for the mouth of the LORD hath spoken it.

Amos 8:4-6. Hear this, O ye that swallow up the needy, even to make the poor of the land to fail, Saying, When will the new moon be gone, that we may sell corn? and the sabbath, that we may set forth wheat, making the ephah small, and the shekel great, and falsifying the balances by deceit? That we may buy the poor for silver, and the needy for a pair of shoes; yea, and sell the refuse of the wheat?

[149] **Q62**. Exodus 20:9. Six days shalt thou labour, and do all thy work:

Exodus 31:15. Six days may work be done; but in the seventh is the sabbath of rest, holy to the LORD: whosoever doeth any work in the sabbath day, he shall surely be put to death.

Leviticus 23:3. Six days shall work be done: but the seventh day is the sabbath of rest, an holy convocation; ye shall do no work therein: it is the sabbath of the LORD in all your dwellings.

[150] Genesis 2:2-3. And on the seventh day God ended his work which he had made; and he rested on the seventh day from all his work which he had made. And God blessed the seventh day, and sanctified it: because that in it he had rested from all his work which God created and made.

Exodus 20:11. For in six days the LORD made heaven and earth, the sea, and all that in them is, and rested the seventh day: wherefore the LORD blessed the sabbath day, and hallowed it.

Exodus 31:17. It is a sign between me and the children of Israel for ever: for in six days the LORD made heaven and earth, and on the seventh day he rested, and was refreshed.

[151] **Q63**. Exodus 20:12. Honour thy father and thy mother: that thy days may be long upon the land which the LORD thy God giveth thee.

Deuteronomy 5:16. Honour thy father and thy mother, as the LORD thy God hath commanded thee; that thy days may be prolonged, and that it may go well with thee, in the land which the LORD thy God giveth thee.

[152] **Q64**. Romans 13:1, 7. Let every soul be subject unto the higher powers. For there is no power but of God: the powers that be are ordained of God.... Render therefore to all their dues: tribute to whom tribute is due; custom to whom custom; fear to whom fear; honour to whom honour.

Ephesians 5:21-22, 24. Submitting yourselves one to another in the fear of God. Wives, submit yourselves unto your own husbands, as unto the Lord.... Therefore as the church is subject unto Christ, so let the wives be to their own husbands in every thing.

Ephesians 6:1, 4-5, 9. Children, obey your parents in the Lord: for this is right.... And, ye fathers, provoke not your children to wrath: but bring them up in the nurture and admonition of the Lord. Servants, be obedient to them that are your masters according to the flesh, with fear and trembling, in singleness of your heart, as unto Christ.... And, ye masters, do the same things unto them, forbearing threatening: knowing that your Master also is in heaven; neither is there respect of persons with him.

1 Peter 2:17. Honour all men. Love the brotherhood. Fear God. Honour the king.

[153] **Q65**. Matthew 15:4-6. For God commanded, saying, Honour thy father and mother: and, He that curseth father or mother, let him die the death. But ye say, Whosoever shall say to his father or his mother, It is a gift, by whatsoever thou mightest be profited by me; And honour not his father or his mother, he shall be free. Thus have ye made the commandment of God of none effect by your tradition.

Romans 13:8. Owe no man any thing, but to love one another: for he that loveth another hath fulfilled the law.

[154] **Q66**. Exodus 20:12. Honour thy father and thy mother: that thy days may be long upon the land which the LORD thy God giveth thee.

Deuteronomy 5:16. Honour thy father and thy mother, as the LORD thy God hath commanded thee; that thy days may be prolonged, and that it may go well with thee, in the land which the LORD thy God giveth thee.

Ephesians 6:2-3. Honour thy father and mother; which is

the first commandment with promise; That it may be well with thee, and thou mayest live long on the earth.

[155] **Q67**. Exodus 20:13. Thou shalt not kill.

Deuteronomy 5:17. Thou shalt not kill.

[156] **Q68**. Ephesians 5:28-29. So ought men to love their wives as their own bodies. He that loveth his wife loveth himself. For no man ever yet hated his own flesh; but nourisheth and cherisheth it, even as the Lord the church.

[157] **Q69**. Genesis 9:6. Whoso sheddeth man's blood, by man shall his blood be shed: for in the image of God made he man.

Matthew 5:22. But I say unto you, That whosoever is angry with his brother without a cause shall be in danger of the judgment: and whosoever shall say to his brother, Raca, shall be in danger of the council: but whosoever shall say, Thou fool, shall be in danger of hell fire.

1 John 3:15. Whosoever hateth his brother is a murderer: and ye know that no murderer hath eternal life abiding in him.

[158] **Q70**. Exodus 20:14. Thou shalt not commit adultery. Deuteronomy 5:18. Neither shalt thou commit adultery.

[159] **Q71**. 1 Corinthians 7:2-3, 5. Nevertheless, to avoid fornication, let every man have his own wife, and let every woman have her own husband. Let the husband render unto the wife due benevolence: and likewise also the wife unto the husband.... Defraud ye not one the other, except it be with consent for a time, that ye may give yourselves to fasting and prayer; and come together again, that Satan tempt you not for your incontinency.

1 Thessalonians 4:3-5. For this is the will of God, even your sanctification, that ye should abstain from fornication: That every one of you should know how to possess his vessel in sanctification and honour; Not in the lust of concupiscence, even as the Gentiles which know not God.

[160] **Q72**. Matthew 5:28. But I say unto you, That whosoever looketh on a woman to lust after her hath committed adultery with her already in his heart.

Ephesians 5:3-4. But fornication, and all uncleanness, or covetousness, let it not be once named among you, as becometh saints; Neither filthiness, nor foolish talking, nor jesting, which are not convenient: but rather giving of thanks.

[161] **Q73**. Exodus 20:15. Thou shalt not steal.

Deuteronomy 5:19. Neither shalt thou steal.

[162] **Q74**. Leviticus 25:35. And if thy brother be waxen poor, and fallen in decay with thee; then thou shalt relieve him: yea, though he be a stranger, or a sojourner; that he may live with thee.

Ephesians 4:28b. But rather let him labour, working with his hands the thing which is good, that he may have to give to him that needeth.

Philippians 2:4. Look not every man on his own things, but every man also on the things of others.

[163] **Q75**. Proverbs 28:19 ff. He that tilleth his land shall have plenty of bread: but he that followeth after vain persons shall have poverty enough. A faithful man shall abound with blessings: but he that maketh haste to be rich shall not be innocent.... He that hasteth to be rich hath an evil eye, and considereth not that poverty shall come upon him.... Whoso robbeth his father or his mother, and saith, It is no transgression; the same is the companion of a destroyer.... He that giveth unto the poor shall not lack: but he that hideth his eyes shall have many a curse.

Ephesians 4:28a. Let him that stole steal no more.

2 Thessalonians 3:10. For even when we were with you, this we commanded you, that if any would not work, neither should he eat.

1 Timothy 5:8. But if any provide not for his own, and specially for those of his own house, he hath denied the faith, and is worse than an infidel.

[164] **Q76**. Exodus 20:16. Thou shalt not bear false witness against thy neighbour.

Deuteronomy 5:20. Neither shalt thou bear false witness against thy neighbour.

[165] **Q77**. Zechariah 8:16. These are the things that ye shall do; Speak ye every man the truth to his neighbour; execute the judgment of truth and peace in your gates:

Acts 25:10. Then said Paul, I stand at Caesar's judgment seat, where I ought to be judged: to the Jews have I done no wrong, as thou very well knowest.

3 John 12. Demetrius hath good report of all men, and of the truth itself: yea, and we also bear record; and ye know that our record is true.

[166] Proverbs 14:5, 25. A faithful witness will not lie: but a false witness will utter lies.... A true witness delivereth souls: but a deceitful witness speaketh lies.

[167] **Q78**. Leviticus 19:16. Thou shalt not go up and down as a talebearer among thy people: neither shalt thou stand against the blood of thy neighbour: I am the LORD.

Psalm 15:3. He that backbiteth not with his tongue, nor doeth evil to his neighbour, nor taketh up a reproach against his neighbour.

Proverbs 6:16-19. These six things doth the LORD hate: yea, seven are an abomination unto him: A proud look, a lying tongue, and hands that shed innocent blood, An heart that deviseth wicked imaginations, feet that be swift in running to mischief, A false witness that speaketh lies, and he that soweth discord among brethren.

Luke 3:14. And the soldiers likewise demanded of him, saying, And what shall we do? And he said unto them, Do violence to no man, neither accuse any falsely; and be content with your wages.

[168] **Q79**. Exodus 20:17. Thou shalt not covet thy neighbour's

house, thou shalt not covet thy neighbour's wife, nor his manservant, nor his maidservant, nor his ox, nor his ass, nor any thing that is thy neighbour's.

Deuteronomy 5:21. Neither shalt thou desire thy neighbour's wife, neither shalt thou covet thy neighbour's house, his field, or his manservant, or his maidservant, his ox, or his ass, or any thing that is thy neighbour's.

Q80. Psalm 34:1. I will bless the LORD at all times: his praise shall continually be in my mouth.

Philippians 4:11. Not that I speak in respect of want: for I have learned, in whatsoever state I am, therewith to be content. 1 Timothy 6:6. But godliness with contentment is great gain.

Hebrews 13:5. Let your conversation be without covetousness; and be content with such things as ye have: for he hath said, I will never leave thee, nor forsake thee.

Luke 15:6, 9, 11-32. And when he cometh home, he calleth together his friends and neighbours, saying unto them, Rejoice with me; for I have found my sheep which was lost.... And when she hath found it, she calleth her friends and her neighbours together, saying, Rejoice with me; for I have found the piece which I had lost.... And he said, A certain man had two sons: And the younger of them said to his father, Father, give me the portion of goods that falleth to me. And he divided unto them his living. And not many days after the younger son gathered all together, and took his journey into a far country, and there wasted his substance with riotous living. And when he had spent all, there arose a mighty famine in that land; and he began to be in want. And he went and joined himself to a citizen of that country; and he sent him into his fields to feed swine. And he would fain have filled his belly with the husks that the swine did eat: and no man gave unto him. And when he came to himself, he said, How many hired servants of my father's have bread enough and to spare, and I perish with hunger! I will arise and go to my father, and will say unto him, Father, I have sinned against heaven, and before thee, And am no more worthy to be called thy son: make me as one of thy hired servants. And he arose, and came to his father. But when he was yet a great way off, his father saw him, and had compassion, and ran, and fell on his neck, and kissed him. And the son said unto him, Father, I have sinned against heaven, and in thy sight, and am no more worthy to be called thy son. But the father said to his servants, Bring forth the best robe, and put it on him; and put a ring on his hand, and shoes on his feet: And bring hither the fatted calf, and kill it; and let us eat, and be merry: For this my son was dead, and is alive again; he was lost, and is found. And they began to be merry. Now his elder son was in the field: and as he came and drew nigh to the house, he heard music and dancing. And he called one of the servants, and asked what these things meant. And he said unto him, Thy brother is come; and thy father hath killed the fatted calf, because he hath received him safe and sound. And he was angry, and would not go in: therefore came his father out, and entreated him. And he answering said to his father, Lo, these many years do I serve thee, neither transgressed I at any time thy commandment: and yet thou never gavest me a kid, that I might make merry with my friends: But as soon as this thy son was come, which hath devoured thy living with harlots, thou hast killed for him the fatted calf. And he said unto him, Son, thou art ever with me, and all that I have is thine. It was meet that we should make merry, and be glad: for this thy brother was dead, and is alive again; and was lost, and is found.

Romans 12:15. Rejoice with them that do rejoice, and weep with them that weep.

Philippians 2:4. Look not every man on his own things, but every man also on the things of others.

Q81. 1 Corinthians 10:10. Neither murmur ye, as some of them also murmured, and were destroyed of the destroyer.

James 3:14-16. But if ye have bitter envying and strife in your hearts, glory not, and lie not against the truth. This wisdom descendeth not from above, but is earthly, sensual, devilish. For where envying and strife is, there is confusion and every evil work.

[172] Galatians 5:26. Let us not be desirous of vain glory, provoking one another, envying one another.

Colossians 3:5. Mortify therefore your members which are upon the earth; fornication, uncleanness, inordinate affection, evil concupiscence, and covetousness, which is idolatry.

[173] **Q82**. Genesis 8:21. And the LORD smelled a sweet savour; and the LORD said in his heart, I will not again curse the ground any more for man's sake; for the imagination of man's heart is evil from his youth; neither will I again smite any more every thing living, as I have done.

Romans 3:9 ff., 23. What then? are we better than they? No, in no wise: for we have before proved both Jews and Gentiles, that they are all under sin; As it is written, There is none righteous, no, not one: There is none that understandeth, there is none that seeketh after God. They are all gone out of the way, they are together become unprofitable; there is none that doeth good, no, not one. Their throat is an open sepulchre; with their tongues they have used deceit; the poison of asps is under their lips: Whose mouth is full of cursing and bitterness: Their feet are swift to shed blood: Destruction and misery are in their ways: And the way of peace have they not known: There is no fear of God before their eyes.... For all have sinned, and come short of the glory of God

[174] **Q83**. Ezekiel 8:6, 13, 15. He said furthermore unto me, Son of man, seest thou what they do? even the great abominations that the house of Israel committeth here, that I should go far off from my sanctuary? but turn thee yet again, and thou shalt see greater abominations.... He said also unto me, Turn thee yet again,

and thou shalt see greater abominations that they do.... Then said he unto me, Hast thou seen this, O son of man? turn thee yet again, and thou shalt see greater abominations than these.

Matthew 11:20-24. Then began he to upbraid the cities wherein most of his mighty works were done, because they repented not: Woe unto thee, Chorazin! woe unto thee, Bethsaida! for if the mighty works, which were done in you, had been done in Tyre and Sidon, they would have repented long ago in sackcloth and ashes. But I say unto you, It shall be more tolerable for Tyre and Sidon at the day of judgment, than for you. And thou, Capernaum, which art exalted unto heaven, shalt be brought down to hell: for if the mighty works, which have been done in thee, had been done in Sodom, it would have remained until this day. But I say unto you, That it shall be more tolerable for the land of Sodom in the day of judgment, than for thee.

John 19:11. Jesus answered, Thou couldest have no power at all against me, except it were given thee from above: therefore he that delivered me unto thee hath the greater sin.

[175] **Q84**. Matthew 25:41. Then shall he say also unto them on the left hand, Depart from me, ye cursed, into everlasting fire, prepared for the devil and his angels:

Galatians 3:10. For as many as are of the works of the law are under the curse: for it is written, Cursed is every one that continueth not in all things which are written in the book of the law to do them.

Ephesians 5:6. Let no man deceive you with vain words: for because of these things cometh the wrath of God upon the children of disobedience.

James 2:10. For whosoever shall keep the whole law, and yet offend in one point, he is guilty of all.

[176] **Q85**. Mark 1:15. And saying, The time is fulfilled, and the kingdom of God is at hand: repent ye, and believe the gospel.

Acts 20:21. Testifying both to the Jews, and also to the

Greeks, repentance toward God, and faith toward our Lord Jesus Christ.

[177] Acts 2:38. Then Peter said unto them, Repent, and be baptized every one of you in the name of Jesus Christ for the remission of sins, and ye shall receive the gift of the Holy Ghost.

1 Corinthians 11:24-25. And when he had given thanks, he brake it, and said, Take, eat: this is my body, which is broken for you: this do in remembrance of me. After the same manner also he took the cup, when he had supped, saying, This cup is the new testament in my blood: this do ye, as oft as ye drink it, in remembrance of me.

Colossians 3:16. Let the word of Christ dwell in you richly in all wisdom; teaching and admonishing one another in psalms and hymns and spiritual songs, singing with grace in your hearts to the Lord.

[178] **Q86**. Ephesians 2:8-9. For by grace are ye saved through faith; and that not of yourselves: it is the gift of God: Not of works, lest any man should boast.

Romans 4:16. Therefore it is of faith, that it might be by grace; to the end the promise might be sure to all the seed; not to that only which is of the law, but to that also which is of the faith of Abraham; who is the father of us all

[179] John 20:30-31. And many other signs truly did Jesus in the presence of his disciples, which are not written in this book: But these are written, that ye might believe that Jesus is the Christ, the Son of God; and that believing ye might have life through his name.

Galatians 2:15-16. We who are Jews by nature, and not sinners of the Gentiles, Knowing that a man is not justified by the works of the law, but by the faith of Jesus Christ, even we have believed in Jesus Christ, that we might be justified by the faith of Christ, and not by the works of the law: for by the works of the law shall no flesh be justified.

Philippians 3:3-11. For we are the circumcision, which worship God in the spirit, and rejoice in Christ Jesus, and have no confidence in the flesh. Though I might also have confidence in the flesh. If any other man thinketh that he hath whereof he might trust in the flesh, I more: Circumcised the eighth day, of the stock of Israel, of the tribe of Benjamin, an Hebrew of the Hebrews; as touching the law, a Pharisee; Concerning zeal, persecuting the church; touching the righteousness which is in the law, blameless. But what things were gain to me, those I counted loss for Christ. Yea doubtless, and I count all things but loss for the excellency of the knowledge of Christ Jesus my Lord: for whom I have suffered the loss of all things, and do count them but dung, that I may win Christ, And be found in him, not having mine own righteousness, which is of the law, but that which is through the faith of Christ, the righteousness which is of God by faith: That I may know him, and the power of his resurrection, and the fellowship of his sufferings, being made conformable unto his death; If by any means I might attain unto the resurrection of the dead.

[180] **Q87**. Acts 11:18. When they heard these things, they held their peace, and glorified God, saying, Then hath God also to the Gentiles granted repentance unto life.

2 Timothy 2:25. In meekness instructing those that oppose themselves; if God peradventure will give them repentance to the acknowledging of the truth

[181] Psalm 51:1-4. Have mercy upon me, O God, according to thy lovingkindness: according unto the multitude of thy tender mercies blot out my transgressions. Wash me thoroughly from mine iniquity, and cleanse me from my sin. For I acknowledge my transgressions: and my sin is ever before me. Against thee, thee only, have I sinned, and done this evil in thy sight: that thou mightest be justified when thou speakest, and be clear when thou judgest.

Joel 2:13. And rend your heart, and not your garments,

and turn unto the LORD your God: for he is gracious and merciful, slow to anger, and of great kindness, and repenteth him of the evil.

Luke 15:7, 10. I say unto you, that likewise joy shall be in heaven over one sinner that repenteth, more than over ninety and nine just persons, which need no repentance.... Likewise, I say unto you, there is joy in the presence of the angels of God over one sinner that repenteth.

Acts 2:37. Now when they heard this, they were pricked in their heart, and said unto Peter and to the rest of the apostles, Men and brethren, what shall we do?

[182] Jeremiah 31:18-19. I have surely heard Ephraim bemoaning himself thus; Thou hast chastised me, and I was chastised, as a bullock unaccustomed to the yoke: turn thou me, and I shall be turned; for thou art the LORD my God. Surely after that I was turned, I repented; and after that I was instructed, I smote upon my thigh: I was ashamed, yea, even confounded, because I did bear the reproach of my youth.

Luke 1:16-17. And many of the children of Israel shall he turn to the Lord their God. And he shall go before him in the spirit and power of Elias, to turn the hearts of the fathers to the children, and the disobedient to the wisdom of the just; to make ready a people prepared for the Lord.

1 Thessalonians 1:9. For they themselves show of us what manner of entering in we had unto you, and how ye turned to God from idols to serve the living and true God

[183] 2 Chronicles 7:14. If my people, which are called by my name, shall humble themselves, and pray, and seek my face, and turn from their wicked ways; then will I hear from heaven, and will forgive their sin, and will heal their land.

Psalm 119:57-64. Thou art my portion, O LORD: I have said that I would keep thy words. I entreated thy favour with my whole heart: be merciful unto me according to thy word. I thought on my ways, and turned my feet unto thy testimonies. I made haste, and delayed not to keep thy commandments. The bands of the wicked have robbed me: but I have not forgotten thy law. At midnight I will rise to give thanks unto thee because of thy righteous judgments. I am a companion of all them that fear thee, and of them that keep thy precepts. The earth, O LORD, is full of thy mercy: teach me thy statutes.

Matthew 3:8. Bring forth therefore fruits meet for repentance:

2 Corinthians 7:10. For godly sorrow worketh repentance to salvation not to be repented of: but the sorrow of the world worketh death.

[184] **Q88**. Matthew 28:18-20. And Jesus came and spake unto them, saying, All power is given unto me in heaven and in earth. Go ye therefore, and teach all nations, baptizing them in the name of the Father, and of the Son, and of the Holy Ghost: Teaching them to observe all things whatsoever I have commanded you: and, lo, I am with you alway, even unto the end of the world. Amen.

Acts 2:41-42. Then they that gladly received his word were baptized: and the same day there were added unto them about three thousand souls. And they continued stedfastly in the apostles' doctrine and fellowship, and in breaking of bread, and in prayers.

[185] **Q89**. Nehemiah 8:8-9. So they read in the book in the law of God distinctly, and gave the sense, and caused them to understand the reading. And Nehemiah, which is the Tirshatha, and Ezra the priest the scribe, and the Levites that taught the people, said unto all the people, This day is holy unto the LORD your God; mourn not, nor weep. For all the people wept, when they heard the words of the law.

Acts 20:32. And now, brethren, I commend you to God, and to the word of his grace, which is able to build you up, and to give you an inheritance among all them which are sanctified.

Romans 10:14-17. How then shall they call on him in whom they have not believed? and how shall they believe in him of whom they have not heard? and how shall they hear without a preacher? And how shall they preach, except they be sent? as it is written, How beautiful are the feet of them that preach the gospel of peace, and bring glad tidings of good things! But they have not all obeyed the gospel. For Esaias saith, Lord, who hath believed our report? So then faith cometh by hearing, and hearing by the word of God.

2 Timothy 3:15-17. And that from a child thou hast known the holy scriptures, which are able to make thee wise unto salvation through faith which is in Christ Jesus. All scripture is given by inspiration of God, and is profitable for doctrine, for reproof, for correction, for instruction in righteousness: That the man of God may be perfect, thoroughly furnished unto all good works.

[186] **Q90**. Deuteronomy 6:16 ff. Ye shall not tempt the LORD your God, as ye tempted him in Massah. Ye shall diligently keep the commandments of the LORD your God, and his testimonies, and his statutes, which he hath commanded thee. And thou shalt do that which is right and good in the sight of the LORD: that it may be well with thee, and that thou mayest go in and possess the good land which the LORD sware unto thy fathers,

Psalm 119:18. Open thou mine eyes, that I may behold wondrous things out of thy law.

1 Peter 2:1-2. Wherefore laying aside all malice, and all guile, and hypocrisies, and envies, and all evil speakings, As newborn babes, desire the sincere milk of the word, that ye may grow thereby.

[187] Psalm 119:11. Thy word have I hid in mine heart, that I might not sin against thee.

2 Thessalonians 2:10. And with all deceivableness of

unrighteousness in them that perish; because they received not the love of the truth, that they might be saved.

Hebrews 4:2. For unto us was the gospel preached, as well as unto them: but the word preached did not profit them, not being mixed with faith in them that heard it.

James 1:22-25. But be ye doers of the word, and not hearers only, deceiving your own selves. For if any be a hearer of the word, and not a doer, he is like unto a man beholding his natural face in a glass: For he beholdeth himself, and goeth his way, and straightway forgetteth what manner of man he was. But whoso looketh into the perfect law of liberty, and continueth therein, he being not a forgetful hearer, but a doer of the work, this man shall be blessed in his deed.

[188] **Q91**. 1 Corinthians 3:7. So then neither is he that planteth any thing, neither he that watereth; but God that giveth the increase.

1 Corinthians 1:12-17. Now this I say, that every one of you saith, I am of Paul; and I of Apollos; and I of Cephas; and I of Christ. Is Christ divided? was Paul crucified for you? or were ye baptized in the name of Paul? I thank God that I baptized none of you, but Crispus and Gaius; Lest any should say that I had baptized in mine own name. And I baptized also the household of Stephanas: besides, I know not whether I baptized any other. For Christ sent me not to baptize, but to preach the gospel: not with wisdom of words, lest the cross of Christ should be made of none effect.

[189] **Q92**. Matthew 28:19. Go ye therefore, and teach all nations, baptizing them in the name of the Father, and of the Son, and of the Holy Ghost:

Matthew 26:26-28. And as they were eating, Jesus took bread, and blessed it, and brake it, and gave it to the disciples, and said, Take, eat; this is my body. And he took the cup, and gave thanks, and gave it to them, saying, Drink ye all of it; For this is my blood of the new testament, which is shed for many for the remission of sins.

Mark 14:22-25. And as they did eat, Jesus took bread, and blessed, and brake it, and gave to them, and said, Take, eat: this is my body. And he took the cup, and when he had given thanks, he gave it to them: and they all drank of it. And he said unto them, This is my blood of the new testament, which is shed for many. Verily I say unto you, I will drink no more of the fruit of the vine, until that day that I drink it new in the kingdom of God.

Luke 22:19-20. And he took bread, and gave thanks, and brake it, and gave unto them, saying, This is my body which is given for you: this do in remembrance of me. Likewise also the cup after supper, saying, This cup is the new testament in my blood, which is shed for you.

1 Corinthians 1:22-26. For the Jews require a sign, and the Greeks seek after wisdom: But we preach Christ crucified, unto the Jews a stumblingblock, and unto the Greeks foolishness; But unto them which are called, both Jews and Greeks, Christ the power of God, and the wisdom of God. Because the foolishness of God is wiser than men; and the weakness of God is stronger than men. For ye see your calling, brethren, how that not many wise men after the flesh, not many mighty, not many noble, are called.

Galatians 3:27. For as many of you as have been baptized into Christ have put on Christ.

1 Corinthians 10:16-17. The cup of blessing which we bless, is it not the communion of the blood of Christ? The bread which we break, is it not the communion of the body of Christ? For we being many are one bread, and one body: for we are all partakers of that one bread.

Q93. Galatians 3:27. For as many of you as have been baptized into Christ have put on Christ.

1 Corinthians 10:16-17. The cup of blessing which we

bless, is it not the communion of the blood of Christ? The bread which we break, is it not the communion of the body of Christ? For we being many are one bread, and one body: for we are all partakers of that one bread.

[192] 1 Corinthians 11:23-26. For I have received of the Lord that which also I delivered unto you, That the Lord Jesus the same night in which he was betrayed took bread: And when he had given thanks, he brake it, and said, Take, eat: this is my body, which is broken for you: this do in remembrance of me. After the same manner also he took the cup, when he had supped, saying, This cup is the new testament in my blood: this do ye, as oft as ye drink it, in remembrance of me. For as often as ye eat this bread, and drink this cup, ye do show the Lord's death till he come.

[193] **Q94**. Matthew 28:19. Go ye therefore, and teach all nations, baptizing them in the name of the Father, and of the Son, and of the Holy Ghost.

[194] Acts 2:38-42. Then Peter said unto them, Repent, and be baptized every one of you in the name of Jesus Christ for the remission of sins, and ye shall receive the gift of the Holy Ghost. For the promise is unto you, and to your children, and to all that are afar off, even as many as the Lord our God shall call. And with many other words did he testify and exhort, saying, Save yourselves from this untoward generation. Then they that gladly received his word were baptized: and the same day there were added unto them about three thousand souls. And they continued stedfastly in the apostles' doctrine and fellowship, and in breaking of bread, and in prayers.

Acts 22:16. And now why tarriest thou? arise, and be baptized, and wash away thy sins, calling on the name of the Lord.

Romans 6:3-4. Know ye not, that so many of us as were baptized into Jesus Christ were baptized into his death? Therefore we are buried with him by baptism into death: that like as Christ was raised up from the dead by the glory of the Father, even so we also should walk in newness of life.

Galatians 3:26-27. For ye are all the children of God by faith in Christ Jesus. For as many of you as have been baptized into Christ have put on Christ.

1 Peter 3:21. The like figure whereunto even baptism doth also now save us (not the putting away of the filth of the flesh, but the answer of a good conscience toward God,) by the resurrection of Jesus Christ.

[195] **Q95**. Acts 2:41. Then they that gladly received his word were baptized: and the same day there were added unto them about three thousand souls.

Acts 8:12, 36, 38. But when they believed Philip preaching the things concerning the kingdom of God, and the name of Jesus Christ, they were baptized, both men and women.... And as they went on their way, they came unto a certain water: and the eunuch said, See, here is water; what doth hinder me to be baptized?... And he commanded the chariot to stand still: and they went down both into the water, both Philip and the eunuch; and he baptized him.

Acts 18:8. And Crispus, the chief ruler of the synagogue, believed on the Lord with all his house; and many of the Corinthians hearing believed, and were baptized.

[196] Genesis 17:7. And I will establish my covenant between me and thee and thy seed after thee in their generations for an everlasting covenant, to be a God unto thee, and to thy seed after thee.

Genesis 17:9-11. And God said unto Abraham, Thou shalt keep my covenant therefore, thou, and thy seed after thee in their generations. This is my covenant, which ye shall keep, between me and you and thy seed after thee; Every man child among you shall be circumcised. And ye shall circumcise the flesh of your foreskin; and it shall be a token of the covenant betwixt me and you.

Acts 2:38-39. Then Peter said unto them, Repent, and be baptized every one of you in the name of Jesus Christ for the remission of sins, and ye shall receive the gift of the Holy Ghost. For the promise is unto you, and to your children, and to all that are afar off, even as many as the Lord our God shall call.

Acts 16:32-33. And they spake unto him the word of the Lord, and to all that were in his house. And he took them the same hour of the night, and washed their stripes; and was baptized, he and all his, straightway.

Colossians 2:11-12. In whom also ye are circumcised with the circumcision made without hands, in putting off the body of the sins of the flesh by the circumcision of Christ: Buried with him in baptism, wherein also ye are risen with him through the faith of the operation of God, who hath raised him from the dead.

[197] **Q96**. Luke 22:19-20. And he took bread, and gave thanks, and brake it, and gave unto them, saying, This is my body which is given for you: this do in remembrance of me. Likewise also the cup after supper, saying, This cup is the new testament in my blood, which is shed for you.

1 Corinthians 11:23-26. For I have received of the Lord that which also I delivered unto you, That the Lord Jesus the same night in which he was betrayed took bread: And when he had given thanks, he brake it, and said, Take, eat: this is my body, which is broken for you: this do in remembrance of me. After the same manner also he took the cup, when he had supped, saying, This cup is the new testament in my blood: this do ye, as oft as ye drink it, in remembrance of me. For as often as ye eat this bread, and drink this cup, ye do show the Lord's death till he come.

[198] 1 Corinthians 10:16-17. The cup of blessing which we bless, is it not the communion of the blood of Christ? The bread which we break, is it not the communion of the body of Christ? For we being many are one bread, and one body: for we are all

partakers of that one bread.

[199] **Q97**. 1 Corinthians 11:27-32. Wherefore whosoever shall eat this bread, and drink this cup of the Lord, unworthily, shall be guilty of the body and blood of the Lord. But let a man examine himself, and so let him eat of that bread, and drink of that cup. For he that eateth and drinketh unworthily, eateth and drinketh damnation to himself, not discerning the Lord's body. For this cause many are weak and sickly among you, and many sleep. For if we would judge ourselves, we should not be judged. But when we are judged, we are chastened of the Lord, that we should not be condemned with the world.

[200] **Q98**. Psalm 10:17. LORD, thou hast heard the desire of the humble: thou wilt prepare their heart, thou wilt cause thine ear to hear:

Psalm 62:8. Trust in him at all times; ye people, pour out your heart before him: God is a refuge for us. Selah.

Matthew 7:7-8. Ask, and it shall be given you; seek, and ye shall find; knock, and it shall be opened unto you: For every one that asketh receiveth; and he that seeketh findeth; and to him that knocketh it shall be opened.

[201] 1 John 5:14. And this is the confidence that we have in him, that, if we ask any thing according to his will, he heareth us.

[202] John 16:23-24. And in that day ye shall ask me nothing. Verily, verily, I say unto you, Whatsoever ye shall ask the Father in my name, he will give it you. Hitherto have ye asked nothing in my name: ask, and ye shall receive, that your joy may be full.

[203] Psalm 32:5-6. I acknowledged my sin unto thee, and mine iniquity have I not hid. I said, I will confess my transgressions unto the LORD; and thou forgavest the iniquity of my sin. Selah. For this shall every one that is godly pray unto thee in a time when thou mayest be found: surely in the floods of great waters they shall not come nigh unto him.

Daniel 9:4-19. And I prayed unto the LORD my God, and

made my confession, and said, O Lord, the great and dreadful God, keeping the covenant and mercy to them that love him, and to them that keep his commandments; We have sinned, and have committed iniquity, and have done wickedly, and have rebelled, even by departing from thy precepts and from thy judgments: Neither have we hearkened unto thy servants the prophets, which spake in thy name to our kings, our princes, and our fathers, and to all the people of the land. O Lord, righteousness belongeth unto thee, but unto us confusion of faces, as at this day; to the men of Judah, and to the inhabitants of Jerusalem, and unto all Israel, that are near, and that are far off, through all the countries whither thou hast driven them, because of their trespass that they have trespassed against thee. O Lord, to us belongeth confusion of face, to our kings, to our princes, and to our fathers, because we have sinned against thee. To the Lord our God belong mercies and forgivenesses, though we have rebelled against him; Neither have we obeyed the voice of the LORD our God, to walk in his laws, which he set before us by his servants the prophets. Yea, all Israel have transgressed thy law, even by departing, that they might not obey thy voice; therefore the curse is poured upon us, and the oath that is written in the law of Moses the servant of God, because we have sinned against him. And he hath confirmed his words, which he spake against us, and against our judges that judged us, by bringing upon us a great evil: for under the whole heaven hath not been done as hath been done upon Jerusalem. As it is written in the law of Moses, all this evil is come upon us: yet made we not our prayer before the LORD our God, that we might turn from our iniquities, and understand thy truth. Therefore hath the LORD watched upon the evil, and brought it upon us: for the LORD our God is righteous in all his works which he doeth: for we obeyed not his voice. And now, O Lord our God, that hast brought thy people forth out of the land of Egypt with a mighty hand, and hast gotten thee renown, as at this day; we have sinned, we have done wickedly. O Lord, according to all thy righteousness, I beseech thee, let thine anger and thy fury be turned away from thy city Jerusalem, thy holy mountain: because for our sins, and for the iniquities of our fathers, Jerusalem and thy people are become a reproach to all that are about us. Now therefore, O our God, hear the prayer of thy servant, and his supplications, and cause thy face to shine upon thy sanctuary that is desolate, for the Lord's sake. O my God, incline thine ear, and hear; open thine eyes, and behold our desolations, and the city which is called by thy name: for we do not present our supplications before thee for our righteousnesses, but for thy great mercies. O Lord, hear; O Lord, forgive; O Lord, hearken and do; defer not, for thine own sake, O my God: for thy city and thy people are called by thy name.

1 John 1:9. If we confess our sins, he is faithful and just to forgive us our sins, and to cleanse us from all unrighteousness.

Psalm 103:1-5. Bless the LORD, O my soul: and all that is within me, bless his holy name. Bless the LORD, O my soul, and forget not all his benefits: Who forgiveth all thine iniquities; who healeth all thy diseases; Who redeemeth thy life from destruction; who crowneth thee with lovingkindness and tender mercies; Who satisfieth thy mouth with good things; so that thy youth is renewed like the eagle's.

Psalm 136. O give thanks unto the LORD; for he is good: for his mercy endureth for ever. O give thanks unto the God of gods: for his mercy endureth for ever. O give thanks to the Lord of lords: for his mercy endureth for ever. To him who alone doeth great wonders: for his mercy endureth for ever. To him that by wisdom made the heavens: for his mercy endureth for ever. To him that stretched out the earth above the waters: for his mercy endureth for ever. To him that made great lights: for his mercy endureth for ever: The sun to rule by day: for his mercy endureth for ever: The moon and stars to rule by night: for his mercy endureth for ever. To him that smote Egypt in their firstborn: for his mercy endureth for ever: And brought out Israel from among them: for his mercy endureth for ever: With a strong hand, and with a stretched out arm: for his mercy endureth for ever. To him which divided the Red sea into parts: for his mercy endureth for ever: And made Israel to pass through the midst of it: for his mercy endureth for ever: But overthrew Pharaoh and his host in the Red sea: for his mercy endureth for ever. To him which led his people through the wilderness: for his mercy endureth for ever. To him which smote great kings: for his mercy endureth for ever: And slew famous kings: for his mercy endureth for ever: Sihon king of the Amorites: for his mercy endureth for ever: And Og the king of Bashan: for his mercy endureth for ever: And gave their land for an heritage: for his mercy endureth for ever: Even an heritage unto Israel his servant: for his mercy endureth for ever. Who remembered us in our low estate: for his mercy endureth for ever: And hath redeemed us from our enemies: for his mercy endureth for ever. Who giveth food to all flesh: for his mercy endureth for ever. O give thanks unto the God of heaven: for his mercy endureth for ever.

Philippians 4:6. Be careful for nothing; but in every thing by prayer and supplication with thanksgiving let your requests be made known unto God.

Q99. 1 John 5:14. And this is the confidence that we have in him, that, if we ask any thing according to his will, he heareth us.

Matthew 6:9-13. After this manner therefore pray ye: Our Father which art in heaven, Hallowed be thy name. Thy kingdom come. Thy will be done in earth, as it is in heaven. Give us this day our daily bread. And forgive us our debts, as we forgive our debtors. And lead us not into temptation, but deliver us from evil: For thine is the kingdom, and the power, and the glory, for ever. Amen.

[207] **Q100**. Psalm 95:6. O come, let us worship and bow down: let us kneel before the LORD our maker.

[208] Ephesians 3:12. In whom we have boldness and access with confidence by the faith of him.

[209] Matthew 7:9-11. Or what man is there of you, whom if his son ask bread, will he give him a stone? Or if he ask a fish, will he give him a serpent? If ye then, being evil, know how to give good gifts unto your children, how much more shall your Father which is in heaven give good things to them that ask him?

Luke 11:11-13. If a son shall ask bread of any of you that is a father, will he give him a stone? or if he ask a fish, will he for a fish give him a serpent? Or if he shall ask an egg, will he offer him a scorpion? If ye then, being evil, know how to give good gifts unto your children: how much more shall your heavenly Father give the Holy Spirit to them that ask him?

Romans 8:15. For ye have not received the spirit of bondage again to fear; but ye have received the Spirit of adoption, whereby we cry, Abba, Father.

[210] Ephesians 3:20. Now unto him that is able to do exceeding abundantly above all that we ask or think, according to the power that worketh in us

[211] Ephesians 6:18. Praying always with all prayer and supplication in the Spirit, and watching thereunto with all perseverance and supplication for all saints;

1 Timothy 2:1-2. I exhort therefore, that, first of all, supplications, prayers, intercessions, and giving of thanks, be made for all men; For kings, and for all that are in authority; that we may lead a quiet and peaceable life in all godliness and honesty.

[212] **Q101**. Psalm 67:1-3. God be merciful unto us, and bless us; and cause his face to shine upon us; Selah. That thy way may be known upon earth, thy saving health among all nations. Let the people praise thee, O God; let all the people praise thee.

Psalm 99:3. Let them praise thy great and terrible name; for it is holy.

Psalm 100:3-4. Know ye that the LORD he is God: it is he that hath made us, and not we ourselves; we are his people, and the sheep of his pasture. Enter into his gates with thanksgiving, and into his courts with praise: be thankful unto him, and bless his name.

213 Romans 11:33-36. O the depth of the riches both of the wisdom and knowledge of God! how unsearchable are his judgments, and his ways past finding out! For who hath known the mind of the Lord? or who hath been his counsellor? Or who hath first given to him, and it shall be recompensed unto him again? For of him, and through him, and to him, are all things: to whom be glory for ever. Amen.

Revelation 4:11. Thou art worthy, O Lord, to receive glory and honour and power: for thou hast created all things, and for thy pleasure they are and were created.

214 **Q102**. Matthew 12:25-28. And Jesus knew their thoughts, and said unto them, Every kingdom divided against itself is brought to desolation; and every city or house divided against itself shall not stand: And if Satan cast out Satan, he is divided against himself; how shall then his kingdom stand? And if I by Beelzebub cast out devils, by whom do your children cast them out? therefore they shall be your judges. But if I cast out devils by the Spirit of God, then the kingdom of God is come unto you.

Romans 16:20. And the God of peace shall bruise Satan under your feet shortly. The grace of our Lord Jesus Christ be with you. Amen.

1 John 3:8. He that committeth sin is of the devil; for the devil sinneth from the beginning. For this purpose the Son of God was manifested, that he might destroy the works of the devil.

215 Psalm 72:8-11. He shall have dominion also from sea to

sea, and from the river unto the ends of the earth. They that dwell in the wilderness shall bow before him; and his enemies shall lick the dust. The kings of Tarshish and of the isles shall bring presents: the kings of Sheba and Seba shall offer gifts. Yea, all kings shall fall down before him: all nations shall serve him.

Matthew 24:14. And this gospel of the kingdom shall be preached in all the world for a witness unto all nations; and then shall the end come.

1 Corinthians 15:24-25. Then cometh the end, when he shall have delivered up the kingdom to God, even the Father; when he shall have put down all rule and all authority and power. For he must reign, till he hath put all enemies under his feet.

[216] Psalm 119:5. O that my ways were directed to keep thy statutes!

Luke 22:32. But I have prayed for thee, that thy faith fail not: and when thou art converted, strengthen thy brethren.

2 Thessalonians 3:1-5. Finally, brethren, pray for us, that the word of the Lord may have free course, and be glorified, even as it is with you: And that we may be delivered from unreasonable and wicked men: for all men have not faith. But the Lord is faithful, who shall stablish you, and keep you from evil. And we have confidence in the Lord touching you, that ye both do and will do the things which we command you. And the Lord direct your hearts into the love of God, and into the patient waiting for Christ.

[217] Revelation 22:20. He which testifieth these things saith, Surely I come quickly. Amen. Even so, come, Lord Jesus.

[218] **Q103.** Psalm 19:14. Let the words of my mouth, and the meditation of my heart, be acceptable in thy sight, O LORD, my strength, and my redeemer.

Psalm 119. Blessed are the undefiled in the way, who walk in the law of the LORD. Blessed are they that keep his testimonies, and that seek him with the whole heart. They also do no iniquity: they walk in his ways. Thou hast commanded us to keep thy precepts diligently. O that my ways were directed to keep thy statutes! Then shall I not be ashamed, when I have respect unto all thy commandments. I will praise thee with uprightness of heart, when I shall have learned thy righteous judgments. I will keep thy statutes: O forsake me not utterly, etc.

1 Thessalonians 5:23. And the very God of peace sanctify you wholly; and I pray God your whole spirit and soul and body be preserved blameless unto the coming of our Lord Jesus Christ.

Hebrews 13:20-21. Now the God of peace, that brought again from the dead our Lord Jesus, that great shepherd of the sheep, through the blood of the everlasting covenant, Make you perfect in every good work to do his will, working in you that which is well-pleasing in his sight, through Jesus Christ; to whom be glory for ever and ever. Amen.

[219] Psalm 103:20-21. Bless the LORD, ye his angels, that excel in strength, that do his commandments, hearkening unto the voice of his word. Bless ye the LORD, all ye his hosts; ye ministers of his, that do his pleasure.

Hebrews 1:14. Are they not all ministering spirits, sent forth to minister for them who shall be heirs of salvation?

[220] **Q104**. Proverbs 30:8-9. Remove far from me vanity and lies: give me neither poverty nor riches; feed me with food convenient for me: Lest I be full, and deny thee, and say, Who is the LORD? or lest I be poor, and steal, and take the name of my God in vain.

Matthew 6:31-34. Therefore take no thought, saying, What shall we eat? or, What shall we drink? or, Wherewithal shall we be clothed? For after all these things do the Gentiles seek:) for your heavenly Father knoweth that ye have need of all these things. But seek ye first the kingdom of God, and his righteousness; and all these things shall be added unto you. Take therefore no thought for the morrow: for the morrow shall take thought for the things of itself. Sufficient unto the day is the evil thereof.

Philippians 4:11, 19. Not that I speak in respect of want: for I have learned, in whatsoever state I am, therewith to be content.... But my God shall supply all your need according to his riches in glory by Christ Jesus.

1 Timothy 6:6-8. But godliness with contentment is great gain. For we brought nothing into this world, and it is certain we can carry nothing out. And having food and raiment let us be therewith content.

Q105. Psalm 51:1-2, 7, 9. Have mercy upon me, O God, according to thy loving-kindness: according unto the multitude of thy tender mercies blot out my transgressions. Wash me thoroughly from mine iniquity, and cleanse me from my sin.... Purge me with hyssop, and I shall be clean: wash me, and I shall be whiter than snow.... Hide thy face from my sins, and blot out all mine iniquities.

Daniel 9:17-19. Now therefore, O our God, hear the prayer of thy servant, and his supplications, and cause thy face to shine upon thy sanctuary that is desolate, for the Lord's sake. O my God, incline thine ear, and hear; open thine eyes, and behold our desolations, and the city which is called by thy name: for we do not present our supplications before thee for our righteousnesses, but for thy great mercies. O Lord, hear; O Lord, forgive; O Lord, hearken and do; defer not, for thine own sake, O my God: for thy city and thy people are called by thy name.

1 John 1:7. But if we walk in the light, as he is in the light, we have fellowship one with another, and the blood of Jesus Christ his Son cleanseth us from all sin.

Matthew 18:21-35. Then came Peter to him, and said, Lord, how oft shall my brother sin against me, and I forgive him? till seven times? Jesus saith unto him, I say not unto thee, Until seven times: but, Until seventy times seven. Therefore is the kingdom of heaven likened unto a certain king, which would take account of his servants. And when he had begun to reckon, one was brought unto him, which owed him ten thousand talents. But forasmuch as he had not to pay, his lord commanded him to be sold, and his wife, and children, and all that he had, and payment to be made. The servant therefore fell down, and worshipped him, saying, Lord, have patience with me, and I will pay thee all. Then the lord of that servant was moved with compassion, and loosed him, and forgave him the debt. But the same servant went out, and found one of his fellowservants, which owed him an hundred pence: and he laid hands on him, and took him by the throat, saying, Pay me that thou owest. And his fellowservant fell down at his feet, and besought him, saying, Have patience with me, and I will pay thee all. And he would not: but went and cast him into prison, till he should pay the debt. So when his fellowservants saw what was done, they were very sorry, and came and told unto their lord all that was done. Then his lord, after that he had called him, said unto him, O thou wicked servant, I forgave thee all that debt, because thou desiredst me: Shouldest not thou also have had compassion on thy fellowservant, even as I had pity on thee? And his lord was wroth, and delivered him to the tormentors, till he should pay all that was due unto him. So likewise shall my heavenly Father do also unto you, if ye from your hearts forgive not every one his brother their trespasses.

Ephesians 4:32. And be ye kind one to another, tenderhearted, forgiving one another, even as God for Christ's sake hath forgiven you.

Colossians 3:13. Forbearing one another, and forgiving one another, if any man have a quarrel against any: even as Christ forgave you, so also do ye.

Q106. Psalm 19:13. Keep back thy servant also from presumptuous sins; let them not have dominion over me: then shall I be upright, and I shall be innocent from the great transgression.

Matthew 26:41. Watch and pray, that ye enter not into temptation: the spirit indeed is willing, but the flesh is weak.

John 17:15. I pray not that thou shouldest take them out of the world, but that thou shouldest keep them from the evil.

[224] Luke 22:31-32. And the Lord said, Simon, Simon, behold, Satan hath desired to have you, that he may sift you as wheat: But I have prayed for thee, that thy faith fail not: and when thou art converted, strengthen thy brethren.

1 Corinthians 10:13. There hath no temptation taken you but such as is common to man: but God is faithful, who will not suffer you to be tempted above that ye are able; but will with the temptation also make a way to escape, that ye may be able to bear it.

2 Corinthians 12:7-9. And lest I should be exalted above measure through the abundance of the revelations, there was given to me a thorn in the flesh, the messenger of Satan to buffet me, lest I should be exalted above measure. For this thing I besought the Lord thrice, that it might depart from me. And he said unto me, My grace is sufficient for thee: for my strength is made perfect in weakness. Most gladly therefore will I rather glory in my infirmities, that the power of Christ may rest upon me.

Hebrews 2:18. For in that he himself hath suffered being tempted, he is able to succour them that are tempted.

[225] **Q107**. Daniel 9:4, 7-9, 16-19. And I prayed unto the LORD my God, and made my confession, and said, O Lord, the great and dreadful God, keeping the covenant and mercy to them that love him, and to them that keep his commandments.... O Lord, righteousness belongeth unto thee, but unto us confusion of faces, as at this day; to the men of Judah, and to the inhabitants of Jerusalem, and unto all Israel, that are near, and that are far off, through all the countries whither thou hast driven them, because

of their trespass that they have trespassed against thee. O Lord, to us belongeth confusion of face, to our kings, to our princes, and to our fathers, because we have sinned against thee. To the Lord our God belong mercies and forgivenesses, though we have rebelled against him.... O Lord, according to all thy righteousness, I beseech thee, let thine anger and thy fury be turned away from thy city Jerusalem, thy holy mountain: because for our sins, and for the iniquities of our fathers, Jerusalem and thy people are become a reproach to all that are about us. Now therefore, O our God, hear the prayer of thy servant, and his supplications, and cause thy face to shine upon thy sanctuary that is desolate, for the Lord's sake. O my God, incline thine ear, and hear; open thine eyes, and behold our desolations, and the city which is called by thy name: for we do not present our supplications before thee for our righteousnesses, but for thy great mercies. O Lord, hear; O Lord, forgive; O Lord, hearken and do; defer not, for thine own sake, O my God: for thy city and thy people are called by thy name.

Luke 18:1, 7-8. And he spake a parable unto them to this end, that men ought always to pray, and not to faint.... And shall not God avenge his own elect, which cry day and night unto him, though he bear long with them? I tell you that he will avenge them speedily. Nevertheless when the Son of man cometh, shall he find faith on the earth?

1 Chronicles 29:10-13. Wherefore David blessed the LORD before all the congregation: and David said, Blessed be thou, LORD God of Israel our father, for ever and ever. Thine, O LORD, is the greatness, and the power, and the glory, and the victory, and the majesty: for all that is in the heaven and in the earth is thine; thine is the kingdom, O LORD, and thou art exalted as head above all. Both riches and honour come of thee, and thou reignest over all; and in thine hand is power and might; and in thine hand it is to make great, and to give strength unto all. Now therefore, our God, we thank thee, and praise thy glorious name.

1 Timothy 1:17. Now unto the King eternal, immortal, invisible, the only wise God, be honour and glory for ever and ever. Amen.

Revelation 5:11-13. And I beheld, and I heard the voice of many angels round about the throne and the beasts and the elders: and the number of them was ten thousand times ten thousand, and thousands of thousands; Saying with a loud voice, Worthy is the Lamb that was slain to receive power, and riches, and wisdom, and strength, and honour, and glory, and blessing. And every creature which is in heaven, and on the earth, and under the earth, and such as are in the sea, and all that are in them, heard I saying, Blessing, and honour, and glory, and power, be unto him that sitteth upon the throne, and unto the Lamb for ever and ever.

1 Corinthians 14:16. Else when thou shalt bless with the spirit, how shall he that occupieth the room of the unlearned say Amen at thy giving of thanks, seeing he understandeth not what thou sayest?

Revelation 22:20. He which testifieth these things saith, Surely I come quickly. Amen. Even so, come, Lord Jesus.

Printed in Great Britain
by Amazon